W9-ARZ-058

Guide Library

Hillwood Museum
Washington, D.C.

VOICES *in the* SNOW

VOICES

RANDOM HOUSE

in the SNOW

Encounters with Russian Writers

B Y Olga Andreyev Carlisle

NEW YORK

FIRST PRINTING

© *Copyright, 1962, by Olga Andreyev Carlisle*
All rights reserved under International and Pan-American
Copyright Conventions. Published in New York by Random
House, Inc., and simultaneously in Toronto, Canada, by
Random House of Canada, Limited. Manufactured in the
United States of America by H. Wolff, New York.

Library of Congress catalog card number: 61–12180

Designed by Ruth Smerechniak

Quotation on page 207: from Nikolai Gogol, *by Vladimir
Nabokov. Copyright 1944 by New Directions. Reprinted by
permission of New Directions, Publishers. On page 35: from*
The Cossacks, *by Maurice Hindus. Reprinted by permission
of Doubleday and Company, Inc. On page 172: from* The
Seven That Were Hanged, *by Leonid Andreyev. Reprinted
by permission of Avon.*

Illustrations by the author

To my mother, Olga Andreyev

Acknowledgments

I wish to thank all the friends in Russia and the United States who inspired and contributed to this book, particularly my editor at Random House, Robert Loomis. I am grateful also to Gloria Loomis and Judith Andreyev, and to Rose Styron, whose collaboration was invaluable in the free poetic translation of Russian poems used in this book, notably those of Osip Mandelstam and Marina Tsvetayeva. I owe thanks also to Robert Lowell for some brief but attentive suggestions concerning the rendering of Boris Pasternak's poems.

CONTENTS

TO LENINGRAD

BORIS PASTERNAK: *Portrait of a Poet*

TO MOSCOW

1 / The Sound
of Russian

Russia! Russia! I see you from the loveliest and most enchanting distance. Everything in you is poor, scattered, inhospitable. . . . Everything in you is vast, bleak, and flat; your squat towns are lost like dots and jots in the middle of vast planes. Nothing beguiles or charms the eye. So what is this secret incomprehensible force driving me towards you?

—NIKOLAI GOGOL, from *Dead Souls*

We were scheduled to arrive in Moscow at about eight o'clock on an evening in January, 1960. I was glad the trip from Prague was a short three hours; after the festive atmosphere of a Swiss flight—pretty hostesses, enormous meals, mounds of chocolate, small pillows—the Soviet plane looked barren and strange, although it was actually a new and powerful jet. The plane was quite empty, since very few travelers venture to Russia in the dead of winter. The other passengers on the flight were men. They had hard, pudgy faces, and for some reason, they gave the impression of slightly theatrical businessmen or possibly Party bosses. They wore felt hats, clutched briefcases, and spoke to each other in hushed but harsh tones of German or Czech. Some of them stared at me across the aisle, not without hostility, I thought. With my light blue coat and black suede boots, I looked conspicuously like a tourist.

We landed on an absolutely flat white expanse broken only by the furrows of shoveled snow on either side of the runway and I could see only a few distant lights on the horizon. But soon faces appeared at the entrance of the plane. They were open, reassuring faces compared to those of my fellow travelers. A hostess and a tall man in a fur hat and long military winter coat greeted us in Russian.

We were to have landed in Vnukovo, the Moscow International Airport, but it turned out that we were in Sheremetievo instead, a smaller airport on the other side of Moscow. The airport personnel were visibly unprepared to receive us, just as we were unprepared to land there. It was particularly awkward for me because my young Muscovite cousin had planned to meet me at Vnukovo. We eventually found out that Vnukovo had been shut down for purposes of disinfection, because there were fears of an epidemic of smallpox. A few weeks before, a painter from Moscow had gone to India, presenting a falsified vaccination certificate. Soon after his return, he became ill. It took a while to identify his illness as smallpox—"black pox," as it is called in Russian. In the meantime, some twenty or thirty people had been contaminated. With a display of efficiency unexpected in a country famed for red tape, the entire population of Moscow, including myself, was vaccinated in a matter of two or three days.

As it turned out, my arrival at this small, out-of-the-way airport made a curiously fitting beginning to my trip. Although Sheremetievo is unprepossessing, it is rustic in a manner which I came to recognize subsequently as typically Russian. There were none of the facilities that make all international airports in the world look alike. On this icy, windswept evening, as we walked from the plane to the airport building, I felt I was in a small outpost lost in the snow. The main building is an old structure, divided into small rooms. Our passports were checked in one, our luggage very casually in another. The rooms were overheated and furnished with stuffed velvet chairs and round tables, their fringed tablecloths reaching almost to the floor. There were yellow tasseled satinette curtains and a portrait of Lenin in each room. Soon after my arrival, I got used to seeing Lenin's stylized, Slavic features, which are displayed everywhere, though Stalin's mustached effigy, more seldom seen and usually hung in less conspicuous places, never ceased to startle me. And it seemed even more malevolent as I learned more about the recent Russian past.

The passport officials, warmly dressed even in the hot room, were sitting at the table checking documents while porters with wide leathery faces stood around in boots and fur hats exchanging jokes. Indeed, everybody seemed relaxed except the young woman with a round, pink face and tightly permanented hair, who sat at the Intourist desk. Since I was the only tourist on the flight—and an unexpected one at that—she had to make special arrangements for my transportation to Moscow. On her desk, along with Intourist travel folders, was a half-empty glass of hot tea and an open volume of *Anna Karenina*. She was reluctant to interrupt her reading, but as soon as I had said a few words, she became intrigued with my accent, and then curious about my clothes. I was fascinated by everything around me, particularly the talk. Until that day, I had only known Russian as the language of an isolated group. Now, loud and slangy, it filled the small airport hall. The faces which I was examining appeared strong and expressive, untouched by the uniform gloss shared nowadays by most Westerners.

A plump young girl came over to the desk. She had just received a telephone message from my cousin, saying he would wait for me at the Byelorussky railroad station in the center of Moscow. It was nine-thirty by then, and he had no way of getting to Sheremetievo. After some delay, the Intourist receptionist arranged for a taxi to drive me into town, while my traveling companions were forced to wait until eleven o'clock for a bus to Moscow.

The taxi driver was a young man with a withdrawn manner. Later, I realized that he simply belonged to the one group of people who always keep their reserve—the Intourist employees. But at that time I was too excited to engage in conversation. Even the sight of the snow was absorbing. Although it may look no different elsewhere, already I sensed that here people lived with the snow, rather than fought it. The whiteness lent an artistic uniformity to the landscape and its inhabitants clad in heavy winter clothes. There was none of the gaudiness which results from prosperity: no bright colors, no clashing of fashions; everybody wore boots, dark overcoats, and fur hats. My first impression was that of stepping into another world, remote in time and place, and yet somehow half-familiar.

We drove through a gray immensity which I had often tried to imagine, particularly after reading *Doctor Zhivago*. The road was covered with hard-packed snow, but the driver was unperturbed. He managed perfectly well without chains, as I subsequently saw all Muscovite drivers do. The road was wide, straight, hardly traveled at all. We rode for fifteen or twenty miles in a frozen landscape broken only by the delicate black patterns of a grove of trees here and there. Then Moscow slowly began to rise before us. First there were eerie, half-finished buildings with huge cranes silhouetted against the sky, and then rows of lighted apartment houses that seemed to extend for miles and miles on either side of the four-lane highway. The road narrowed, became a street, and the houses grew smaller; dimly lighted by infrequent street lamps, they looked unbelievably ancient. There were high banks of snow on the sidewalks. I had my first glimpse of one of the odd but characteristic sights of Moscow—bundled women, big and heavy, with shovels and brooms, clearing the pavement in the night. As we neared the center of town, we passed broad classical façades. Finally, we turned into the wide plaza in front of the Byelorussky station, a half-moon building with white stucco columns all around it.

I hadn't seen my cousin in several years—he had studied in the West but now was majoring in medicine at the University of Moscow—but I recognized him easily. He seemed hardly changed since we had seen each other last. He clung to his Western habit of not wearing a hat, and it was a wonder that his ears hadn't frozen in the cold as he stood waiting outside. He had wanted to make sure we didn't miss each other. He greeted me and I noticed his Russian had grown more harsh and colloquial in comparison with our own soft-spoken family accent.

He got into the taxi with me and we drove off to the Hotel Metropole. My cousin told me I was fortunate to have been assigned to this hotel since it is near the center of town.

Tourists were often made to stay at the Ukraine, a long way from the city proper, which is a serious disadvantage in winter when the cold may be so penetrating that even a few steps outside are torture.

The Metropole is a prerevolutionary hotel, a sprawling building occupying a whole block, with its main entrance on the square of the Bolshoi Theater. I was soon to discover, however, that the Metropole had a bad reputation with Muscovites. Until recently certain members of its personnel were believed to be police agents. I heard several times that there were periods in the Stalin regime when one visit by a Russian to the Metropole was enough to bring about his arrest. In those years, the great majority of Moscow's foreigners resided there. Something of a disquieting aura still surrounds the Metropole. One finds oneself wondering: Could some of the hotel maids have been government agents at one time? And what about now?

Two bronze Chinese sculptures stand at each side of the entrance to the hotel. These remarkably ugly barking dogs seem to warn the visitor of the possible risks to be run. As a matter of fact, some of my older friends were reluctant to venture inside the hotel, although no one among the young people I knew ever had any hesitation about meeting me there, whether in my room or in the café downstairs. Every day, the lobby of the Metropole was crowded until mid-evening. Young Muscovites and foreigners appeared to mingle there quite freely.

The restaurant and the café were already closing when we got to the Metropole but we were able to buy some fruit sodas and pastries and then went upstairs to my room on the second floor. It was large and rather somber, but it had deep comfortable chairs and it was warm and quiet. Two tall double French windows were draped in heavy lace and gray brocade, completely isolating one from the outside world. The outer window had a little hinged pane to let in the air. Through it I could see a narrow white courtyard shut off by a brick wall etched with snow. The wall looked ancient —eighteenth century perhaps, judging by the pattern formed by the bricks. The room was softly lighted by beautiful bronze Empire lamps incongruously provided with dowdy beaded shades. Those shades, Victorian and impractical, are extremely common in Russia. In one of the large portraits of Stalin at the Metropole—several were lurking there in dark corners along the main staircase—he is studiously bent over a desk lit by two such lamps. Throughout my stay, each time I struggled with those shades, trying to get enough light to write or read by, I involuntarily thought of Stalin.

Soviet hotel rules specify that no visitor is to stay in a guest's room after midnight, but we drank our sodas and ate the oversweet cakes and talked late into the night without any interference. I was delighted to see that my cousin looked happy, that he had lost none of his spirit. It was heartening to see somebody, linked to oneself by many common childhood memories, clearly well-adjusted to this strange city.

My cousin was full of curiosity: what had brought me to the USSR? I had written only that I was coming to Moscow, and he was bewildered about why I had made the trip in the middle of winter. I explained to him that a small American literary magazine, the *Paris Review*, had asked me to come to the Soviet Union to interview various authors for a series they were running entitled Writers at Work. I had made no arrangements in advance concerning these interviews. I was counting on the fact that my father had renewed many family and literary ties during a trip in

1957, and that these contacts would aid me. It seemed preferable to improvise a plan of action after getting to Moscow rather than to write in advance and risk being dismissed at once or at best have to seek the help of a ponderous institution called the Cultural Service, which was set up to help foreigners. Now that I was here I wanted to find out everything at once. Would the Soviet writers be willing to talk to me at all? What was Pasternak's situation after the attacks of his colleagues of the Writers' Union? How could I meet Mikhail Sholokhov? I was interested in painting too. Did my cousin have young painters among his friends? Did he go to many art shows? These were some of the questions I asked him while in turn he asked about New York and Paris, about our friends and our relatives. I also gave him the presents I had brought: some heavy sweaters from Switzerland, a couple of records of Italian operas and a skiing cap. He must have given this cap away, for afterward he remained bareheaded as before.

I had undertaken the *Paris Review* assignment with the hope that it would be possible to call on Soviet writers and to talk to them about their work with a fair measure of freedom. But as we sat in this unfamiliar quiet room, drinking strange-tasting soft drinks, I had sudden doubts about this. After all, I would be considered a foreigner, from the West. However, little by little, as we talked, I began to sense that my cousin found my projects interesting, not in the least bizarre or subversive. Finally he got up and started walking slowly around the room. He spoke thoughtfully: "You might find it difficult to obtain interviews on the subject of writers at work," he said. "Describing the techniques of their writing will seem odd to some Soviet writers—as you know, the Russian emphasis is on subject matter rather than on form . . . and if they do say anything, you may find they're simply restating the doctrine of socialist realism. Perhaps if you approached your assignment in a broader perspective—let yourself be guided by what interests the Russian writers themselves—you might then hear all sorts of things worth recording for the American reader."

If necessary I was willing to be just a listener but there were many questions I wanted to ask too. Where did tact begin for a foreigner in the USSR? My cousin remained silent for a few minutes; he was clearly trying to answer as accurately as he could. After a moment he spoke, warming up to the subject as he went on: "Right now the Soviet Union is undergoing more changes than you can imagine. As a result, you will encounter contradictory attitudes, hear contradictory opinions from equally well-informed, intelligent people. My own impression is that you will have some fear to face. This is the worst enemy of the Soviet Union, this fear that many people—rather understandably —have kept from less happy years. You will find, however, that it affects almost exclusively those who have suffered at the hands of Stalin. But then, who can tell for sure about the future? At least the arbitrary abuses of Stalin's time have altogether faded from our lives.

"I, for one, am optimistic. If you listen and look and use your intuition you'll be able to see and hear things whose existence you had never suspected," he continued. "Russian voices are anxious to make themselves heard nowadays. Times have changed radically since Stalin's death, you know. Generally speaking, people have no reason to be shy of foreigners—as long as they do not feel that those foreigners are actively opposed to the Soviet way of life. The Communist Party, the supreme authority here, is undergoing changes too. It is turning again to what it was once—a body in which every member has a voice . . ."

I was fascinated by all this, and listened in silence hoping that he would say more about Soviet politics, but his tone became lighter as he went back to my immediate future: "Moscow is full of life right now. I'll take you to the theater to see Mayakovsky's *Bed Bug*, and you must attend a poetry reading. As for the writers you mentioned, Pasternak, so I hear, leads the life of a recluse, and some of us feel that he is altogether an eccentric. I have never been to his house, but it is said that he is very much wrapped up in himself, that he speaks about himself for hours, that he is a little bit crazy, perhaps . . . Actually, nothing prevents you from going to Peredelkino and calling on him; he has been known to be sympathetic to younger people. Sholokhov is a different problem; many a journalist has traveled to the Don country to sit on his doorstep without managing to get as much as a glimpse of him. But the most original, the most talented people of all, in my opinion, are right now the younger poets of Moscow . . ." Excitedly, he told me of the popularity of public poetry reading. I had attended some readings in Paris, given by émigré poets, but it was hard to imagine the huge gatherings he described.

That night, I lay in bed with my first Moscow insomnia. The bed was one of those weirdly put together Russian beds whose secret I hadn't yet discovered. The bedding is not tucked in—blankets and sheets are folded like envelopes on top of each other. The bed looks normally made, but one is assured of incessant drafts unless the whole thing is completely redone. It didn't matter anyway. I was exhilarated; I couldn't sleep. I had reached Russia, the remote but omnipresent force of my childhood. And Moscow lay outside my windows, silent and sleeping yet festive in its whiteness.

2 / A Parisian Childhood

Heureux qui, comme Ulysse, a fait un beau voyage,
Ou comme cestuy là qui conquit la toison,
Et puis est retourné, plein d'usage et raison,
Vivre entre ses parents le reste de son aage!

Quand revoiray je, helas, de mon petit village
Fumer la cheminée, et en quelle saison
Revoiray je le clos de ma pauvre maison,
Qui m'est une province, et beaucoup d'avantage?

Plus me plaist le sejour qu'ont basty mes ayeux,
Que des palais Romains le front audacieux,
Plus que le marbre dur me plaist l'ardoise fine:

Plus mon Loyre gaulois que le Tybre latin,
Plus mon petit Liré que le mont Palatin
Et plus que l'air marin la douceur angevine.
                    —JOACHIM DU BELLAY, "Les Regrets," 1558

My father, Vadim Leonidovich Andreyev, a Russian citizen, left Russia for France in 1919 and was unable to revisit until 1957. He is the oldest son of Leonid

Andreyev, and is himself a poet. On his mother's side he is
a great-great-nephew of Taras Shevchenko, the Ukrainian
national poet. In my mother's family are several generations
of revolutionaries. Her grandfather, Elie Kolbassin, was a
nobleman of liberal tendencies as well as a friend of Turgenev and a distinguished man of letters. The conflict between revolutionary ideas and an aristocratic, traditional
way of life was particularly strong among the Kolbassins.
Turgenev depicted this conflict in *Father and Sons* and some
of the characters in the novel were modeled after members
of the Kolbassin family.

Leonid Andreyev died in Finland in 1919, but he was
still a vivid presence in my family when I was a child. I also
came to know him through the many photographs we had
of him. He was exceptionally handsome in a romantic way—
he had dark eyes, somehow cold and yet sensitive. His photo-
graphic poses were dramatic, but his portraits never looked
affected, although others of that time often do. He appeared
plunged in a meditative gloom, which was photogenic, often
wearing dashing costumes—evening clothes or traditional
Russian shirts and boots or a sea captain's uniform. He had
had a passion for the sea and for a while he owned a yacht. In
several pictures he wore a black velvet jacket, a favorite
garment which gave him a slightly theatrical, medieval air:
he resembled the duke out of his own play, *Black Masks*.
There were several photographs of him taken with Maxim
Gorki, my father's godfather, who was for a long time
Andreyev's very dear friend. These two faces, intent and
alive, were part of my childhood world. Tolstoi and Block
were also there—faces as familiar as those of relatives—
Tolstoi, as he was painted towards the end of his life, bare-
foot with a walking stick, and Block, a beautiful, emaciated
face in a red velvet frame over my father's desk.

In the thirties, my father received a few Andreyev heir-

looms from Finland, where he had grown up. Andreyev
had built a house outside of Russia on the Black River,
across the gulf from St. Petersburg: because of his liberal
ideas, he and his family felt safer there. Now the house had
to be sold. It was a huge log mansion impossible to keep up
after the Revolution. Later, during World War II, the whole
Black River area was razed and burned; only three trees
remain today of the elaborate grounds which surrounded
Andreyev's oversized home, built in a Scandinavian style, and
full of carved Gothic furniture and immense tile wood-
burning stoves. At least four servants were required to keep
them going in wintertime.

In the last years of his life, Leonid Andreyev was isolated from St. Petersburg and all of Russia. By 1918 the
Russo-Finnish border was closed. Lonely and ill, Andreyev
analyzed in his journal his own motives in building his house,
so characteristic of the solemn and melancholy Russian
nineteen hundreds. "In building this enormous house in the
desert, as if on the edge of the land of Canaan, I wanted to
create a beautiful life, severely devoted to tragedy. To be
outside of society, of routine—and I found myself outside
of life as well, throwing my writings into life once in a
while, like a boy throwing stones over a fence into a stranger's garden . . . Peter the Great did me in. He cut a window open onto the sea and I sat near it to admire the view
from the shore and now I drift away. Finland! Why am I
in Finland? Of course my attraction for the sea is part of it.
Then there is the proximity of St. Petersburg, of publishing houses and theaters, and of writers. I had a vague
thought: to be near a boundary, in a neutral, unengaged
zone . . ."

Less than a year later he died, still completely cut off
from Russia.

Out of Andreyev's massive and numerous possessions,

manuscripts were saved and sent to us, as well as large paintings and drawings in dark frames, two bronze candelabras, an inkwell, and ashtrays whose turn-of-the-century monumentality contrasted with our small modern apartment. Indeed those things looked as if they had come from another world—and they did. For a time, we had on the wall of our living room a picture by Andreyev, who had been a talented draftsman. It was an enlargement of Goya's *Devils Cutting Their Toenails* made in dark gray and green chalks. I strongly objected to these devils; they were removed before long and the wall restored to its pastel lightness. Goya seemed alien at that time; although Russian intellectuals in Paris were poor and life was often hard but it was peaceful. We lived in a world not unlike that of the French impressionists: only the Spanish Civil War cast a slowly spreading Goyaesque shadow on our existences, foreboding the war to come.

I grew up not far from Paris, near the Vallée de Chevreuse, much of which was then pastoral, practically unchanged since the eighteenth century. There were rolling hills, ancient farms, and half-abandoned châteaux, as in old landscape engravings showing formal French parks softly merged with the woods.

When I learned to ride a bicycle at the age of six, my father took me on excursions around Chevreuse. Much of it is hilly, but if he pushed me uphill I was able to go on the longest trips. I came to know every small road in the valley and in the adjoining Forêt de Verrières, a renowned hunting ground in the Renaissance. The stylish, self-contained grace of these landscapes has vanished.

Le Plessis seemed far out of Paris then. We lived in a newly built middle-income development—a "garden city," as it was called, where certain apartments had adjoining artists' studios. Many young painters and sculptors were living nearby. The *cité jardin* was located on the edge of a park, and in summertime it was full of wild flowers. We led a quiet life. Trips to Paris were rare for the children. I remember vividly being taken once to the literary Dôme when I was five or six—the poets reading their poems and arguing, and my first whiff of the unique smell of a Parisian café.

During the thirties, the majority of my parents' friends were Russians living in Paris. Not that France was inhospitable; we had French friends too, and during the war years we were especially close to them. Yet I grew up in an essentially Russian atmosphere. On Sundays, many of my parents' friends came for the day to Le Plessis—poets and painters who often traveled from Paris on their bicycles. We took long walks in the countryside. In the fall we went mushroom-gathering; in the summer we became berry pickers. There was afternoon tea-drinking, conversations that lasted late into the night, and poetry readings which I could overhear from my room after I had been put to bed. I loved to hear poetry recited. My father reads beautifully—his own verse and classical poetry—and so did Marina Tsvetayeva, who was a close friend, and came often to see us before her return to Russia in 1938, when she could no longer bear her exile. She looked like a thin gypsy and her hair was turning white against her very dark skin. She had a slightly hooked nose, wore heavy silver jewelry, and smoked incessantly. Boris Poplavsky, perhaps the most original among the poets who formed the Russian School of Paris and as yet undiscovered by literary critics, read his verse with a singing, nasal voice:

> *On a summer day above the white sidewalks,*
> *Paper lanterns were suspended.*

> *A trumpet's voice rasped, over the avenue*
> *Flags dreamt on their long poles.**

Sometimes Poplavsky arrived at our house on foot, having walked all the way from Paris to Le Plessis. He usually wore knickers and a snap-brim plaid cap. Dark glasses protected his very pale blue eyes, which looked strained from reading or staying up late. I was always happy to see him: he and the poet Nicholas Tatichteff, a friend who often came with him, admired the drawings I had done with the tinted paper and pastels my father had given me.

I heard learned, lengthy conversations on all sorts of esoteric subjects, incomprehensible to me then, but captivating in their vagueness. Poplavsky had read everything, including the most arcane, peculiar books—Nostradamus, Jules Verne and treatises on the Cabala. He was a bohemian, had many friends, mostly Russian artists from around Montparnasse, and they are still fanatically devoted to Poplavsky's memory. He died in the middle nineteen-thirties of an overdose of narcotics, probably accidentally: he took drugs in the company of a friend and apparently this man, who was bent on suicide, didn't hesitate to involve the poet.

Poplavsky was the only Russian poet of the Paris School to be directly influenced by the French poetry of that period. Russia never figures literally in his poems while Paris is always there, a fanciful, nostalgic city. He was a kind of Russian Guillaume Apollinaire, dead too soon, and there is a legend around his name, as if his poems and himself were of one essence. As a child, I thought that he was a perfect incarnation of a poet.

Of course, trips to Paris were always special occasions. When I was seven or eight years old I recall Alexei Remizov in his Parisian apartment reading Gogol's *Vii*, a story of

---

* From *Flags*, 1931, published in Russian in Paris.

witchcraft. How menacing it sounded in the dusky room! Remizov and his wife, Seraphima Pavlovna, my godmother, rarely went out. We visited them in Auteuil, on Rue Boileau, in a place full of old Russian objects—beadwork, embroidery, icons. Every day Remizov worked until four o'clock in the afternoon. The curtains were usually drawn, and the walls glittered with Remizov's weird, cubistic collages and his drawings of creatures, half-animal, half-human. The house was populated by invisible presences: fairy-tale characters, small bizarre animals, mythical spirits. Alexei Remizov told their stories to his guests; children and adults alike were introduced to his imaginary friends. His intimates were invited to join the "Council of Apes," a fanciful society over which he presided, and to which many well-known Russian writers belonged at one time or another.

My godmother was very religious, and the Remizovs' house was disquieting with its little oil lamps, red and blue, hanging in front of icons. It was all darkness and glitter with the feeling of secret happenings behind closed doors as in an orthodox church. The Remizovs constituted a world in themselves, as profoundly Russian as anything I have ever known. As a writer, Remizov lived in a continual contact with the Russian past, which was his favorite subject matter.

When I was older, I was occasionally taken to Berdyaev's house in Clamart, a Parisian suburb. On Sundays, before and after World War II, he held informal philosophical discussions. He had the rare gift of bringing together antagonistic groups from the Emigration—Greek Orthodox priests, socialists, and anarchists—as well as French intellectuals like Emmanuel Mounier and Jacques Maritain. In springtime, Berdyaev's home looked like a Bonnard painting, with its French windows and chestnut trees in pink bloom standing very close to the house.

Nicolas Berdyaev had been a Marxist in his youth. He

turned to Christianity in later years, and became a considerable force in modern existentialist philosophy. His works deal with the significance of the creative act, his best-known book being a brilliant study of Dostoevsky. He received visitors from all over the world; at his house one met Tibetans, Americans, Icelanders. And he was always open to new ideas. In the middle forties, I remember in particular a conversation at his house concerning Henry Miller. Berdyaev asserted that the American writer (then little known by Europeans) had expressed better than anyone else the nature of our times—chaos breaking into the orderly ways of the past.

Berdyaev—who was half French—was an aristocratic-looking man out of an earlier, more elegant era. His eyes and thick eyebrows were very dark and he wore a black velvet beret on his long gray hair. He had a nervous twitch near his mouth, but one quickly got used to his raising his hand to hide it. His manners, his hospitality, were intimately courteous and yet simple; he knew the art of putting people at ease, drawing out the shyest guest, the most modest visitor from a distant country. I suppose that of all the Russian intellectuals whom we knew, Berdyaev was the most cosmopolitan—or rather, he had a Russian nineteenth-century kind of universality, like Pushkin, whose "Renaissance spirit" Berdyaev especially admired.

In the early and middle thirties, my parents saw the writer Isaac Babel whenever he came to Paris, usually in the summer. They were close to Babel, who had encouraged my father as a writer. In fact, my father's first book of poems was published under Babel's sponsorship. Babel often urged my parents to go back to Russia and even tried to help them obtain a visa to the USSR. To him Stalin was the strong but good master whom Russia needed then.

Babel and my father once undertook a motorcycle trip along the Seine, down to Rouen and Le Havre, to see the riverside landscapes described by Maupassant. At the end of their journey they spent long hours in bars in the port at Le Havre, sipping cider and listening to the conversations of seamen. Babel was delighted; he enjoyed watching simple people of any nationality. I remember the pleasure he got from a visit to a colony of Cossacks who had settled on a farm not far from Paris, where they managed to lead a primitive existence similar to the one they had known on the banks of the Dnieper. He told endless tales about those Cossacks, improvising new episodes as he went along. He was a marvelous, lyrical raconteur, but as a writer he was slow and rewrote his stories a great many times, striving for an absolute perfection. Babel's output was considered insufficient. Once, Ilya Ehrenburg had to speak for his friend at a Soviet Writers' Union meeting: "I am myself like a rabbit and can produce books by the litter," said Ehrenburg. "Babel works slowly—like an elephant he carries his baby for two years . . . the result is worth it."

Babel loved Russia and the Russian language above everything. Life abroad was impossible for him, although his wife and daughter lived in Paris. He appreciated the devotion in our family to the Russian language, which had been preserved in its purity over the years, and it disturbed him that his daughter Natasha spoke Russian with a French accent.

I remember him vividly—his myopic eyes behind thick lenses, intelligent, attentive, sad but with sudden flarings of gaiety. Babel's jokes, always unexpected, were irresistible. Children loved him. His "sad eyes" are remembered in my family because of a story he often told: During the Civil War, he fought in the Red cavalry under General Budenny.

No one knew Babel was a Jew, which was just as well in a time when the average soldier or Cossack was apt to be fanatically anti-Semitic. But once, after an exhausting, bloody attack, he stopped near a well for a drink of water. Sorrow and fatigue gave him away, Babel recounted; his origin was perceived in his "sad Jewish eyes." A cavalryman bent over him and hissed: "You dirty Jew."

His passion for observing and associating with all types of people finally betrayed Babel. In 1938, he was arrested for alleged black-market activities. Soon after his arrest Babel perished and with him his unpublished manuscripts, including a novel on which he had worked for years.

My parents, of course, knew a great many Russian painters in Paris: Soutine, Pougny, Larionov, Goncharova, and others. The artists were usually happier than the poets; the Emigration had brought them to the artistic capital of that time. Fedor Rojankovsky, who later became one of the best-liked juvenile artists in America, lived next door to us in one of the studios of the *cité jardin*. He gave costume parties and kept squirrels and hedgehogs in his studio. Small, quick, dark-eyed, he himself resembled a squirrel. He sketched incessantly and often asked us children to pose for him. We were rewarded with nuts or cakes or a new box of colored pencils.

I had thought that the faces Rojankovsky drew were overstylized, exaggeratedly Slavic. But in Russia I discovered that they truly are the prevalent Russian type: wide-faced, fair, blue-eyed. Somehow the intellectuals we knew were often of a different type—olive-skinned with an aquiline nose, not unlike the faces in the Russian medieval paintings.

All the Russians in Paris shared an immense nostalgia— almost a metaphysical longing for their country. Russians lived in secluded groups outside of French daily life, and it was hard to survive both materially and spiritually. The intellectuals and the artists tended to gather around Montparnasse and the Latin Quarter. With very few exceptions, they suffered from being cut off from "Russian Reality," as they naïvely called the little they knew of events which were taking place in Russia then. Actually, the Parisian Russians helped maintain the stream of Russian culture, which dwindled in the Soviet Union during the rigorous thirties.

Yet the Parisian writers had been humble, forlorn. Few survived. To my surprise, I discovered in Russia that the Russians of Paris concerned the Soviet intellectuals a great deal. Boris Pasternak wanted to hear all about them and asked for their books. A prominent Soviet doctor, a passionate collector of paintings, even paid tribute to the women in the Emigration! To him, painting was the measure of a civilization: "I often think that the Revolution, which sent abroad so many Russian women, performed a good service. Those Russian women made superlative wives for the painters in Paris. They contributed to the spreading of the best of our spirit . . ."

Because of my family's literary background, my Soviet friends tended to regard me as a compatriot. In turn, in this new environment, I experienced moments of recognition—of *déjà vu*. Those moments were the result, no doubt, of literary echoes. It was to Dostoevsky, for example, one of the less descriptive of Russian novelists, that I owed many of my flashes of recognition—of houses, of streets, of people. All that I had read made Leningrad in particular immediately understandable. The city is breath-takingly beautiful, and yet subdued and sad. More than anywhere else, I felt there this peculiarly Russian trait—a longing for Europe and the Latin world. Leningrad was still St. Petersburg, Peter's single-handed creation. Peter was hoping to open a window to the West for Russia. His city still stands, an opulent monument to the Russian urge to communicate with Europe. It was all the more poignant to me because I had known from childhood all about the Russian's inability—or unwillingness—to survive outside of a Russian world, real or imagined. The West had held no answers for the majority of Russians who ventured outside their country in the great turmoil of the Revolution.

3 / Muffled Moscow

I

The bell towers are ringing
Somewhere in the Kremlin
Somewhere in my homeland
Somewhere

Towers are ringing
Abandoned, ringing
Where on this earth?
My home
My slumber
Laughter
Light
Of narrow feet, the footsteps . . .

II

Then lift my hands
Empty now
Through the black window
And fling me down
Through the midnight clanging
Of the clock tower
Home. I would go home
Like this: head down
From the noisy tower. Home

Not against the cobblestoned square
But into the rustling whispering
Wings of my warrior.
Archangel,
Wait for me
There.

—MARINA TSVETAYEVA, *Separation,* 1921

During my first days in Moscow the weather was gray, the city looked like a nineteenth-century engraving. The ever fresh snow and the dark bundled figures of the Muscovites emphasized the city's resemblance to a black and white print. The women with wicker brooms patiently swept the snow off the pavement. And occasionally, a miniature, motor-driven snow plough cleared the sidewalks. A rather thin, slow line of traffic circled noiselessly around Bolshoi Square. It was not particularly cold outside and I went for frequent walks in the vicinity of the hotel. Once in a while, a ray of sun made the fresh snow sparkle. Everything looked exotic to me and yet so well known that I couldn't believe my eyes: so this was the quiet city, the composed people who were my lost home? Almost any new city seems a little forbidding at first, except perhaps for those which are safely dead—Florence, for instance. But progressively, one learns to interpret the inhabitants' manner, their gestures. These people, however, were Russians, I knew their language, and mistakenly I expected to find them at once understandable. My feeling of estrangement lasted for several days. Only as I started to make friends in Moscow did I begin to feel at ease in the crowd, which was reserved, even-mannered, with a remarkable lack of aggressiveness and considerable dignity. Only once or twice unexpected and violent outbreaks of rudeness reminded me of tales about the coarseness of the revolutionary years. I soon realized that Moscow was a metropolis, a true capital despite the fact that it seems parochial by comparison with New York or Paris. One sensed that this was the main gathering point in an enormous area, whose inhabitants did not look up to any other city. On the contrary, they were in the center of the world—a boundless plain where great forces had focused precisely in Moscow.

One of the things that struck me at once was how gentle people were to their children. I saw children taken everywhere, to stores and museums, or strolling through the city. It was near the end of the New Year's vacation, and yet there was none of the wild clamoring which is a trademark of many American children on an outing. Nor did I notice any feeling of intimidation, which all too often characterizes French children. Toddling through the Moscow streets, these creatures, bundled like teddy bears, made one think of children at their best: childlike and yet responsible and quiet. The smaller ones were charming to watch: rosy-faced, they wore fur coats and long mufflers tied behind their backs. They smiled back readily at a stranger. Perhaps the Russian child, who appears as a rule so poised and stable, is a product of a family linked closely by tradition and by necessity.

Walking through the sinuous side streets of the heart of Moscow, where one still finds many log houses and odd-shaped yards, I came across small churches, some of which were open. Once in a great while, an elderly Muscovite might be seen inconspicuously shuffling in or out of one. Several of the buildings were in the process of restoration— as historical monuments rather than places of worship. Those churches intensified the old-fashioned aspect of Moscow. Small and wooden, with peeling golden cupolas, they were surrounded by decrepit carved fences. Despite the fact that they had been allowed to go to ruin they still seemed a part of everyday life, as were the chimes of a distant church bell, which I faintly heard one evening. I was told that those were the bells of Novodevichy monastery on the outskirts of Moscow whose churches are still open. Subsequently, I went there to look for the tomb of my paternal grandmother, Alexandra Andreyeva. There was so much snow in the small cemetery that I wasn't able to find her tomb, but the deserted monastery itself, built in a kind of Russian "flamboyant Gothic"—an extravagant mixture of light stone and pink brick—seemed a fairy castle lost in the barren white landscape.

The Kremlin was usually the goal of my walks. The little churches on my roundabout way were only a reminder of the marvels of the Kremlin, where my cousin had taken me on my first day in Moscow. Coming up from the quay of the Moskva River we went in through one of the tower gates. I had never seen a fortress like the Kremlin before: it sprawls casually and yet is solidly belted by monumental brick fortifications, whose ornate designs, so Russian in character, were delicately outlined in snow. The formidable crenelated towers guarding the gates are half-Asian, half-European. The Kremlin, closed to the public for almost thirty years, is open now. From the depths of Russia, viewers come, filling it from morning until the closing hour at night. Just outside the fortress on Red Square, they form in long shuffling files waiting to see their leader lying in state. The people's faces reflect wonderment, reverence, and a certain relieved curiosity: "Here is the stronghold of those who ruled us for so long . . ." (Squeamish, I never ventured inside the mausoleum: it is a grim-looking structure and the quiet crowd waiting to enter was awesome in its composure.)

Along with a dense crowd of people, we walked up the Kremlin hill toward its center, the Cathedral Square. There was a sudden burst of sunshine. All the cupolas of the Kremlin churches above us shone at once with their various shades of gold and silver. I was overwhelmed. The heart of Russia was glistening in the sun. When we reached the inner square it was flooded with yellow sunshine—the sky and the shadows were a purplish blue. Built in the fifteenth and sixteenth centuries by Italian architects and their Russian pupils, the square is an intimate fusion of Italian and Russian styles. Several cathedrals are grouped there to form what was once the center of Orthodox Russia. The Cathedral of the Assumption is the most elegant and the holiest to the faithful, a shrine for the miraculous Virgin of Vladimir, whose intervention is said to have prevented the invading Tamerlane the Great of Samarkand and his horde from sacking Moscow in 1395. The Archangel's Cathedral, consecrated to the Archangel Michael, Marina Tsvetayeva's Warrior, equals it in graceful strength.

Every church on the square subjects the viewer to the spell of its perfect proportions, although the buildings stand there in seeming disorder. We walked around the square, entering each church in turn; then we looked down toward the glistening Moskva River. The Tartar hordes followed its valley in the Middle Ages, and the Kremlin was built and fortified in an effort to stop them. We walked along the eighteenth-century Senate building which now houses the Supreme Soviet, and then out of the fortress by way of the enormous Savior's clock tower, which serves as the main entrance to the Kremlin. The sun was setting; it made the dark red brick walls glow. And we could admire one of the celebrated sights of Moscow, a sunset behind the Cathedral of St. Basil. It was an orange and golden sunset. The clustered cupolas of St. Basil, half bright Easter eggs, half tulip blossoms, were outlined in black against the sky. We walked around the church, and the multicolored designs of its walls and the painted cupolas reflected the sun in patches. Because

of the light automobile traffic, the plazas and the avenues of
the center of Moscow give a feeling of spaciousness; and the
snow emphasizes this. Red Square was a phantasmagorical
snow field illuminated by the sunset.

I went back to the Kremlin many times. I walked around
its churches, looked for hours at the newly cleared frescoes,
primitive and forceful, and at the icons. The icons of the
Kremlin are at present undergoing an intense program of
cleaning and restoration. From beneath layers of candle
smoke and overpainting, they emerge in their primeval
beauty: luminous colors, powerful compositions, simplified
shapes. I had not expected to find that icons were such a
markedly national art: the airiness of Russian icons differen-
tiates them from other Byzantine art works. I was surprised
by their monumentality. I had an émigré child's conception
of an icon—that of a family treasure, a small painting which
is hung on the right side corner of the main room as you
enter it. In reality, icons may be immense, whole panels en-
closing an altar.

I could not exhaust the Kremlin's wonders and always
went away with a certain feeling of dissatisfaction at not
being capable of absorbing more. I regretted that I was unable to organize in my mind the things that I saw. Although
strictly Russian in character, they encompassed an immense
variety of styles and decors—the snow and the freshly
gilded cupolas, the translucent tones of the icons, the frescoes and the multicolored tiles are all intertwined in my
memory. I am sure that this slightly dazzled fascination is
the very effect that Orthodox churches, with their mixture
of pomp and informality, are calculated to produce.

As I went around the Kremlin I thought of Tsvetayeva
in the wintry starved Moscow of the early twenties. I understood Tsvetayeva better as I came to know Moscow: she was

a true Muscovite, even her speech as I recall it was from Moscow, slightly guttural. I imagined Alexei Remizov as a child, going to church in the Kremlin. He described himself in his books, a small boy from a Moscow merchant's family, living in a muffled, deeply traditional world. For him the churches of the Kremlin and those of the St. Andronic monastery (an ancient monastery now restored to serve as a museum of icon master Andrei Rublev's school) were a revelation in sound and color. The colors were those of the icons, the gold of the candles, the people's Sunday clothes all blurred by his myopic vision into a marvelous and frightening symphony. The sounds were the bells of Moscow's innumerable bell towers, roaring for hours on end on Easter Sunday. Their solemn brass song was part of the same ominous symphony as the colors—and both shaped Remizov as an artist.

Remizov has the reputation of being a difficult writer, and it is true that he devoted all his life to exploring the Russian language. This led him back to the seventeenth century, which he considered to be the point of high blossoming of Russian, not yet adulterated by foreign superimpositions. But Remizov was essentially a modernist, and as such he had the unfortunate quality of exasperating the average person. All his life he sought new ways of expressing the real—he was a realist in the same sense as Gogol was, endowed with the ability to convey the tangible world, concrete and terrifying. His descriptions of his childhood recreated old Moscow for me long before I actually saw it.

SHOLOKHOV:

Portrait of a Cossack Writer

4/"You Have Come Home"

The Ukraine was Russia's great Wild West, with no force other than a benevolent nature and a vengeful Mohammedan tribesman to threaten life and endanger liberty. Up north Czars and boyars and a landed gentry were snuffing out the last vestiges of popular freedom. The Russian State was becoming more closely knit, more authoritarian, more autocratic, more contemptuous of the common man's right. But Moscow had not yet laid a crushing hand on these faraway lands in the South. Here were no masters of the earth. Here no one had yet arrogated power and privilege unto his autocratic self. Here the common man—fugitive, serf, vagabond, nonconformist, bandit, whoever he might be, whatever his social and racial origin—might still assert his will and profess the dignity of his person.

—MAURICE HINDUS, from *The Cossacks*

It is hard for us in the West even to imagine Mikhail Sholokhov's fame in the USSR. Russian writers are lionized and he is the best-known novelist in the country.

In the last thirty years the once illiterate masses of the vast Soviet republics have taken avidly to books, and Sholokhov has become an almost legendary figure to them. The Don country which he describes is indeed like the American West. It has something of the same historical significance. It is a frontier country: the word Ukraine comes from *Okraïna,* "border" in Russian. Until the Revolution the Cossacks of the Ukraine retained certain privileges and had more freedom than the rest of the Russians. Their country was the scene of many uprisings against the power of the Czars. It is an immense expanse of open land with a relatively mild climate. Their horses are fast and their women beautiful. Like our cowboys, they are said to be independent and proud.

Sholokhov is himself a Cossack and Cossack life inspires his books. His reputation is reminiscent of Hemingway's: he is a virile writer, but tenderness underlies his toughness. In the wide gray panorama of Soviet socialist realism, there is something unique about *And Quiet Flows the Don.* It is a book of great conviction. It conveys better than any other the cruelty of the Russian Civil War. It is epic, rich, simple, yet many-sided. *And Quiet Flows the Don* tells of the incredible sufferings endured by Russians, and more specifically by Cossacks, in a way that is understandable and moving, while the statistics of those years are either meaningless or unbearable. Somewhere in this immense novel there is a scene in which Gregor, the harsh, unimaginative hero, has just sabered to death four Red sailors. He collapses, falls to the ground, and in a moment of stunned awareness he shrieks what is the theme of any civil war: "Whom have I killed"?

The histories of most nations are bloody, but Russian history, with its succession of invasions and of dictators, is perhaps the bloodiest. It is almost as if Russia had been fated to an extreme and absurd cruelty. This fate Sholokhov has captured especially well in his novel.

Sholokhov's reputation as a writer of talent and insight is unanimously recognized in Moscow literary circles. The fact that he did not publish anything for more than twenty years, as if in silent protest against Stalin's excesses, is sometimes pointed out with sympathy. He is reported to have spoken out against those among the members of the Writer's Union who attacked Pasternak after he was given the Nobel Prize. He is known to be the *enfant terrible* of the Writer's Union, where he keeps his colleagues intimidated by his directness. Some say that he is full of his own power, a difficult man. During his trip to the United States with Khrushchev, Sholokhov was hostile and even rude at times, especially to journalists. He was unimpressed with American achievements and outspoken about it. He is said to be contemptuous of the Soviet literary milieu. Not one among my acquaintances in the literary world knew Sholokhov personally. I was advised not even to make an attempt to meet him; why risk unpleasantness?

But besides my admiration for *And Quiet Flows the Don*, the fact that Sholokhov was unattainable intrigued me. A few days after my arrival, when I heard that Sholokhov was in Moscow attending the Supreme Soviet, I decided that I should at least try to make his acquaintance. As an excuse I had an informal query for him from his New York publisher, Alfred A. Knopf, who had not yet received the last chapters of *Harvest on the Don*. I was asked to look into the matter if I could manage to get in touch with Sholokhov. No one seemed to know where he was staying, although he was said to have an apartment in Moscow. At first it seemed impossible even to find out his telephone number. There are no up-to-date phone books in Moscow, and a completely inadequate information service. The fact that many apartments are shared further complicates telephone listings. Finally, after several days, I managed to get the telephone number of his secretary. It was given to me by a friend who had secured it from one of Sholokhov's translators. My friend was sworn to secrecy by the translator, who didn't want anybody to know that he had divulged the number. Sholokhov's hostility toward having his privacy intruded upon was intimidating, but now that I had his number I thought I might as well use it. So I called up the secretary one morning from my hotel room. The telephone was answered by a polite young man who had Sholokhov call me right back.

Sholokhov had a brisk voice. He was curt but civil as he promised to look into the Knopf question. His clear, slightly ironic intonation made me increasingly uncomfortable. Just as I was beginning to lose my original daring, Sholokhov, as an afterthought, did precisely what I had initially hoped he would do. He asked me to stop by the Hotel Moskva, where he was staying temporarily. I felt unnerved when he hung up. Something in Sholokhov's manner made me doubtful that he would want to talk to me about his writing.

The working of one's memory is unpredictable. Right after our telephone conversation, I suddenly remembered a story about Sholokhov which I had completely put out of my mind. It was related to me by a former schoolmate, who had gone to Moscow to attend the Youth Festival in 1957. Along with many British students she sailed from London on *The Molotov* (subsequently renamed *Baltika*), which was to bring Premier Krushchev to New York in 1960. Sholokhov had traveled on *The Molotov* from Stockholm to Helsinki. He was rumored to have visited Stockholm in connection with the Nobel Prize, which some thought might be given to him that year. It was midsummer, the time of "white nights," when the nights are so short in northern latitudes that it never really gets dark. Most of the passengers were full of gaiety and anticipation, but Sholokhov was a sullen presence; he refused to meet his fellow travelers or the crew, with the exception of the lower echelons of the ship's staff. To them he allegedly made a speech about *Not by Bread Alone*, a novel by Vladimir Dudintzev just then published, which had been criticized in certain official Soviet circles. Sholokhov said that the book wasn't worth reading—a badly written book. According to the ship's librarian, every copy available was immediately borrowed as a result of this declaration. (Although *Not by Bread Alone* is not outstanding from a literary point of view, it is noteworthy in that it is one of the first published criticisms of the ruling Soviet bureaucracy. Eventually Khrushchev defended it against charges of anti-Communism, adding colloquially that "he didn't have to prick himself with pins to stay awake at night and finish the novel.")

I could imagine Sholokhov as my friend had described him, moodily pacing the deck, looking toward the sea—a hard sunburnt face with a white mustache profiled against the summer sky. His entourage was also on deck: several people standing in a small, awe-struck group.

My desire to meet Sholokhov vanished as I thought of this episode. I began to think of all the pleasant things I could have done that evening: I could have gone to the Obraztsov puppet show, or to the Bolshoi. I was certain my encounter with Sholokhov was doomed to failure. For the first time I felt like an unwanted outsider.

Despite the prospect of a forbidding evening, the day

progressed agreeably. The snow fell incessantly; Moscow was gray and mysterious. It was a good day to go around the Kremlin again, a little less crowded than usual because of the weather. I went through its churches with a painter who was an expert on Russian antiquity. Then we had tea near the Kremlin, at the Café National, Moscow's most urbane meeting place. I forgot about literary assignments, Sholokhov and the Don Cossacks.

Toward evening the snow stopped falling. The city was buried in deep whiteness but the intrepid Moscow taxis still made their way through the streets; they went very slowly and even the soft noises of a northern city had completely faded away. It was less cold than usual, a rather exhilarating evening full of glistening street lights. As I drew closer to the Moskva, however, I became aware of that special apprehension which takes over just before a visit to the dentist, when all hopes for a miracle to prevent the dreaded ordeal have collapsed.

The Moskva is just halfway between the Metropole and the Kremlin. It is a huge mass of polished dark gray granite separated from the Kremlin's walls by a wide esplanade. Russians, rather than tourists, stay in this severe hotel. I made my way to Sholokhov's suite without stopping at the desk, since he had given me its number. Taking a deep breath, I knocked at the door and a voice said to come in. The room was large, typical of Soviet hotel rooms. Yellow curtains screened off the sleeping area. There was a rug with a dark red and blue pattern, a round dining table covered with a white cloth, and a serving table near it laden with bottles and fruit.

Two men sitting at the table got up as I came in. I recognized Sholokhov from his photographs, but he was older and somehow milder-looking than I expected. I introduced myself, and Sholokhov presented me to his companion, a dark, rather heavy young man who turned out to be Sholokhov's Italian publisher. After he'd introduced us, Sholokhov said, "I asked you to come by so that Mr. Giuseppe Levi might explain to you about the last chapter of my book. You must also join us for some supper. But first tell me why you speak Russian with such an odd intonation . . ." As I sat down I said the usual things about my background, that my grandfather was Leonid Andreyev, that I was French. I thought that Sholokhov looked slightly relieved. Perhaps he had expected me to be more businesslike, more of a professional literary lady.

I welcomed a glass of vodka which was offered me, and Sholokhov offered a reassuring toast, something like "Welcome to our literary-minded guests." Then I asked the Italian publisher about the last chapters of *Harvest on the Don*. Sholokhov sat back and listened. He was a short man, dressed in riding pants and high black boots and a navy turtleneck sweater. His hair and mustache were a grayish white. There was a mixture of vitality and military stiffness in his carriage, and he created an impression of authority; was it perhaps due to his success, to his always finding himself in a commanding position? Yet his manner was direct and it put me at ease. I felt there was no need to try to prove myself, because in any case Sholokhov—for better or for worse—was able to see beyond one's social manners. Despite age and war and politics, and whatever eroding forces shape a middle-aged man in a country like the USSR, he had an open smile and eyes of extraordinary brilliance. They were blue, inquisitive, intelligent. I imagine that they could be icy, but at that moment they had an amused expression. He had the smiling Russian eyes of which Turgenev speaks.

Looking at Sholokhov I recalled a state of mirth which frequently affects his characters: they are shaken by inner laughter. Sholokhov was silently laughing just then, and I gathered that he was laughing at both the Italian publisher and me as we tried to speak in Russian about *Harvest on the Don*. My own Russian becomes hesitant when I feel intimidated, and the publisher's was not very good at all. However, I understood that the Italians were temporarily delaying the American publication of Sholokhov's novel in order to establish for themselves the world copyright.* The ending of the book was soon to be sent to New York.

Finally Sholokhov could not contain himself any longer and he burst into loud laughter. This gaiety is what I will always remember about him; it turned a formal encounter into a convivial evening. As a writer and as a person, Sholokhov epitomizes the tradition of Southern Russian folk humor of which Gogol is the master. Much of Gogol's comic genius disappears in translation; similarly, it is hard to convey Sholokhov's sense of humor, which is based on a subtle and whimsical use of language. Shchukar's delightfully mad monologues are quite lost in the English translation of *Harvest on the Don*.

I had read Gogol and Sholokhov but I had never actually heard their kind of Russian spoken. What in Sholokhov's writing seems at times a trifle too mannered and folksy comes to life in his speech, where each sentence is wrought as a small poetic phrase. His laughter was warm and I had to join in. Mr. Levi laughed too. Then Sholokhov began

---

* Since the Russians have not yet signed the Universal Copyright Convention or the Berne Convention, Russian books are not protected by copyright outside of the USSR. Certain Soviet writers allow a foreign publisher to establish world copyright for them outside the USSR. They are thus protected for the foreign editions of their works.

teasing him. He told a long, complicated story about World War II; how in 1943 a battalion he was covering as a war correspondent was surrounded by Italians. The Italians' artillery was absolutely inaccurate. It never even got near a target. Italians are no warriors, said Sholokhov. One felt sorry for them when the blockade was broken, and half-frozen Italians who should never have ventured into the Russian winter were made prisoners. Perhaps fearing that he had offended Mr. Levi, Sholokhov interrupted his tale to propose a toast to him and to today's Italy.

When dinner was ordered I had my first taste of Cossack hospitality. Russians as a whole are considered very hospitable, but the southern Russians—Ukrainians, Cossacks, Georgians—are the most hospitable of all. Their generosity, which can be overwhelming, sometimes even terrifying, was marvelously described by Gogol.

Two waitresses in white uniforms came in at Sholokhov's call. It was clear that they knew Sholokhov was a famous writer and they had no doubt read *And Quiet Flows the Don* and wept over the tale of the ill-starred love between Aksinia and Gregor. They addressed Sholokhov as Mikhail Alexandrovich. Sholokhov joked with them as they took his order and brought in plates of hors d'oeuvres. They were both intent on providing us with the best possible dinner. The older waitress was quite motherly. She repeated softly the word *koushaïty*—do eat please—over and over, and soon Sholokhov was seeing to it that Mr. Levi and I followed her injunction. Before long we were fighting off new helpings, additional glasses of wine and vodka and Caucasian champagne. It was necessary for me to alternate between Soviet vodka and coffee, which I had discovered was the only way to remain lucid throughout a long Russian evening. It worked well only if I didn't gulp a full glass of vodka at each toast. Taking a small sip, however, is not good form: one is coaxed into emptying a glass each time and there is no end to toasts. If I were a man I wouldn't have gotten away with sips, but ladies are not really pressed into drinking. Mr. Levi, of course, had to comply with Sholokhov's hospitality. Sholokhov himself drank a lot of vodka but he seemed unaffected by it except that he became more expansive. A softness came over his eyes.

As we slowly consumed the dinner—caviar, consommé with meat puffs, several lavish dishes of meat and fish— Sholokhov told stories about Leonid Andreyev. Not first-hand ones, because he had not known him personally. Andreyev was no particular literary favorite of his, but he seemed to have a great deal of sympathy for him, perhaps because of Andreyev's friendship with Gorki, a relationship well known in the USSR. Gorki, of course, is considered the foremost Soviet novelist of his generation, the father of socialist realism.

Sholokhov remembered that it was at Andreyev's apartment in Moscow that the Central Committee of the Bolshevik Party was arrested in 1903. Andreyev was also arrested at that time and spent several months in prison although he was never a Bolshevik.

"Do you know what it is to drink 'like Andreyev'?" Sholokhov asked. "It has become a Russian expression. You set a line of small glasses of vodka along the edge of a table and drink them one after the other without stopping: one, two, three. Obviously you have not inherited Andreyev's talent for drinking!"

He spoke of Gorki and of his gigantic funeral, and of how he had not seen him for many years before his death because of the way he had treated Maria Fedorovna Andreyeva (no relation to our family). She was a well-known actress who lived with Gorki for several years. She accompanied him to America in 1906 and there was a scandal when it was discovered that she was not married to him. "Andreyeva had given everything for Gorki and the Revolutionary cause—her husband, her career, her money. And then Gorki left her, turned away from her. I could never quite forgive him."

I was particularly interested in hearing Sholokhov speak about Andreyeva. My father remembers her distinctly, although he knew her only when he was a very small child. Gorki was devoted to my grandmother, whom he called "Lady Shura" (Shura is a Russian diminutive of Alexandra), and when she died in 1908, my grandfather and my father, who was then five years old, went to stay with Gorki and Andreyeva in Capri. On their arrival, Andreyeva presented my father "all at once with more toys than he ever had in all his life."

As the conversation progressed I began to feel what was to be the theme of my acquaintance with Sholokhov. Unlike many of my new friends, especially the younger ones, he had no use for anything at all Western, but he was curious about a Russian born and brought up in a foreign country. Sholokhov is a chauvinist, which is by no means rare among Russian writers. It was even true to some extent of my grandfather, and certainly of Dostoevsky, who particularly despised everything French and German. From the 1830's to the end of the century the Slavophiles demanded a return to old Russian roots and fought the impact of Western ideas on Russian society.

"Even though I traveled in an official capacity, and make allowances for the fact that I was in the United States as a member of Nikita Sergeevich's escort and was therefore unable to see much of everyday life, I didn't like what

American civilization has done to people. From what I could tell there is a lack of love for simple endeavors. It makes life senseless. Everything, including people's work and their leisure, is mechanized. Perhaps it is not so in France; one may be direct and casual and walk around and talk to anyone in the street, make friends with working people. I should like to take a trip to France and see how the simple people live there. But I really want to stay in Russia . . ."

From several things that he said, it seemed clear that Sholokhov was well read, particularly in Russian, but he is one of those writers who deliberately avoids literary topics. I asked him on several occasions who his favorite authors were and he always answered with a joke. Nor did he respond any better to inquiries about his own work.* On the other hand, he was anxious to speak about people he had known, to listen to descriptions of persons and situations out of everyday life.

He made sweeping statements about the West such as, "All Western literature is effeminate." And it was useless to argue or to invoke writers like Hemingway or the younger

---

* Here is the exact recording of a laconic literary exchange:
Q: Mikhail Alexandrovich, please tell me about the circumstances in which you wrote *And Quiet Flows the Don*?
A: It was so long ago that I forget anything about the circumstances, the atmosphere, my mood when I wrote this novel.
Q: How do you see the future of Russian literature? What themes, what forms do you foresee?
A: The future of Russian literature I expect to be brilliant—but the forms—future only will tell.
Q: How do you conciliate the activities of a writer with those of a Deputy?
A: To conciliate those activities both complicates creative work and enriches it, as it provides new material for a writer . . .
Q: What Russian writers do you love best?
A: Love? I love only women . . .

generation of American novelists, because he wasn't that interested. But about Russia and Russians he was perceptive and lyrical. It was no affectation; he loved them with an open and irrepressible love. I have seldom encountered a more earthy yet haunting feeling for Russia. Sholokhov's world as a writer and as a man is not intellectual; neither is it spiritual, although it is poetic. No one in Russia in his generation has caught so well the nostalgia of fleeting time. Sholokhov's realm is that of the sentiments and, even more, that of the elusive sensuous perception. The finite nature of the moment as he describes it causes a certain melancholy to pervade his writings. His conversation was full of concrete touches, tangy and yet tender. Through Remizov, I had heard spoken Russian raised to the level of an art. Remizov had a special sense for words and for syntax. But then, he was a medievalist, a man of immense culture and his conversation was often elliptic and even archaic. Sholokhov's was as effective in an entirely different way: free-flowing and yet exact and sharp. Its expressiveness captivated me and I regret my inability to convey it.

The desire to show the best of his country overcame what would have been a very understandable feeling—especially on the part of a man so prominent in Soviet official circles—that of mistrust towards a foreigner. I did not sense any reserve on Sholokhov's part. He was as free in his conversation as any of my younger friends. I sat spellbound as he rambled from subject to subject. People and landscapes and long-past war episodes were brought to life, full of vivid details. Mr. Levi was fascinated too, even though some of the more colloquial and colorful parts of Sholokhov's stories must have escaped him. Interrupting himself occasionally to fill our glasses, Sholokhov told us about the Don country.

"Some day I should like you to come to the Don country in summertime," he said. "You'll go swimming in the river. One shore of the Don is high, a chalky cliff, the other is sandy and low, full of warm little pools of brilliant blue water where one can let oneself float for hours. Our summer is gorgeous, the best time to visit. Fruits are plentiful. There are melons and cucumbers and tomatoes, the sweetest in all the country. Fishing is at its best in summertime. It's paradise for a child: you should bring your son, Olga Vadimovna."

He also spoke of the lovely Don spring and of the birds in early summer, of swans settled on the lakes like scattered pearls and drakes calling from the deep blue marshes along the Don River. Then in the fall, high-flying geese gave their sad call way above the steppe.

On an impulse he decided that we should come to Veshenskaia as soon as the Supreme Soviet was over to see the Don country under snow. "Giuseppe, you must come with your wife. And you must come too, Olga Vadimovna. Let's take an evening train to Rostov-on-the-Don and then from there we'll fly in a small plane to Veshenskaia. We shall go hunting along the frozen river. You will have to borrow warm clothes; what you are wearing is ridiculous city garb —but that can be easily arranged. Felt boots, sheepskin coats . . . You must see the people and their houses, see the white windy steppe and breathe some Russian air. The steppe is so beautiful in wintertime, all smooth, you must see its breath-taking vastness."

It was late, perhaps two o'clock, when I went back to the Metropole. The city was completely asleep, deserted except for the reassuring shimmer of street lights. As I had said good-bye, Sholokhov led me to one of the tall double windows. It opened into the back of the big modern hotel. Characteristically, there was a tilted ancient wooden building in the courtyard—some old house now used as a shed, but lovely and mysterious in the faint moonlight. "Look at the snow," said Sholokhov, "there is no snow like this anywhere else, and it is yours. You have come home."

5 / The Moods of a Cossack

Our good earth is not cut with ploughs,
Horses hoofs cut it deep;
It is sown with the heads of our Cossacks.
Our Don is graced with many young widows,
And flowered with many young orphans.
The waves of our Don are swollen with tears.
"O dear father, quiet Don,
Why do you flow so troubled and dark?"
"Cold springs rise from my depths,
And a fish all white troubles my heart . . ."

       –Cossack song of the time of the Civil War, as quoted by MIKHAIL SHOLOKHOV in *And Quiet Flows the Don.*

When I left Sholokhov's hotel that snowy night I had no expectation of seeing him again. I thought of that evening as a completed, slightly dreamlike sequence. Sholokhov's warmth, his tales about the Cossack country, the snow outside—it almost seemed to me that I had seen the Don, after hearing it evoked so lovingly in Sholokhov's words.

The meeting of the Supreme Soviet lasted longer than

was expected, however, and Sholokhov, to my happy surprise, sometimes telephoned me, usually in mid-evening when I was back at the hotel after an exhausting day. I always had the hope of catching up on sleep, but I knew that if I went to bed early I would toss around for several hours, kept awake by too much excitement and too much strong tea consumed during the day. My head was filled with too many new ideas. So when Sholokhov telephoned I would accept his invitation and stroll over to the Moskva for a short call.

People were always visiting with him in the evening. For the most part they were writers less well established than he. As Deputy to the Supreme Soviet, however, Sholokhov was approached with a great variety of pleas. All kinds of people ask a Deputy to speak for them to the authorities. In some cases there are requests for political (and even criminal) rehabilitation, or, because Sholokhov is such a prominent author, he is often asked for a recommendation to a publishing house. Quite a few people somehow found Sholokhov at the Moskva. I suspect that it was in order to escape them that he changed hotels in the middle of the session of the Supreme Soviet and went to stay at the Budapest, a smaller hotel known for its good restaurant.

Sholokhov was always sympathetic to those who did manage to see him. Thus he was helpful to a middle-aged poet, slightly nervous and anxious to please, who recited a great deal of his satirical verse during an evening. The man had just been divorced and had no place to go. An apartment is the hardest commodity of all to obtain in Moscow. Sholokhov telephoned someone at once and was given a promise of prompt attention. Like many well-known writers, Sholokhov seemed caught between his interest in people—and no doubt his need for their admiration—and his desire for solitude.

I discovered during those evenings that Sholokhov was

not just a raconteur; he could listen as well. He loved to stay up late and entertain his guests, his eyes full of inner laughter. A visit to Moscow enabled him to meet and observe a great variety of people. He would make them talk while he was being hospitable, ordering food, opening new bottles. To the consternation of the waitresses he used what must be the Cossack manner, slapping the bottles on the bottom with his hand until the cork slipped out, instead of using a corkscrew. Sholokhov was attentive to his guests. If he is full of himself, as is often said—and the adulation with which he is surrounded would easily turn nearly anyone into an egomaniac—it is not apparent. He possessed the novelist's essential gift of being genuinely interested in someone—if only for the length of an evening—not for the purpose of having his own ideas confirmed, but rather to see something new through that other person.

Considering that his phone number was a secret, Sholokhov received a great many calls in the space of an evening. Finally he would unplug the telephone. This is a current practice in Moscow, and the state-owned company does not object to it. Many of these calls came from journalists who wanted to interview Sholokhov in connection with *Harvest on the Don*, which had just been serialized in *Pravda*. Sholokhov took a dim view of journalists in general ("parasites," he once said of them in his definitive manner). But one journalist was part of his entourage for a couple of evenings. Eugene was the closest to an "average" Soviet citizen whom I met in the limited world which I explored in Moscow. This fact in itself made him interesting to me.

My introduction to Eugene was unusual. At Sholokhov's invitation I went over to the Moskva one evening around nine o'clock. When I entered I noticed a young man who was talking on the telephone in a corner of the room. I could not see his face. With great intensity he was reading something from a typewritten manuscript. Sholokhov asked me to sit down. He himself was absorbed in listening. After four or five minutes I gathered that what was being read was precisely the last pages of *Harvest on the Don,* which had brought about my meeting with Sholokhov.

I had read the first volume, called *Seeds of Tomorrow.* (*Seeds of Tomorrow* and *Harvest on the Don* are published under the general title, *Virgin Soil Upturned.*) Davidov, the main hero who appears in the first volume, is a Party-bred factory worker, a former sailor of the Baltic who comes to the Don in the thirties to direct the collective farm of Gremyachy Log. He is a thoughtful, resolute man of good will but often clumsy and unaware of the complexity of his task. From what was being said into the telephone, I realized that Davidov dies at the end. The young man was reading a passage in which Davidov's friends are visiting his grave. Soon the reader's voice began to tremble with emotion. He was reading artlessly, but the thought of Davidov's death moved him. I was moved too. It was a beautiful passage:

"White clouds still floated above Gremyachy Log, but now they were autumnally packed in the high sky faded with the hot summer; the leaves of the poplars above the river were streaked with gold, the water in the stream was translucent and icy. Fostered by the meager autumn sun, a fragile pale green grass sprang on the graves of Davidov and Nagulnov. And there was even some unknown steppe flower trying belatedly to assert its poor life, huddling against the palisades of the fence around the graves. Nearby three sunflower shoots swayed gently whenever the wind blew low."

When the young man finished, Sholokhov introduced him. Eugene was a reporter on the staff of *Izvestia*, edited by Alexei Adzhubei, who is Khrushchev's son-in-law and a personal friend of Sholokhov's. Sholokhov explained that Eugene had been reading to his wife in the Urals who had been anxiously waiting to hear the novel's ending. Eugene was thirty or thirty-five years old, slim, tall, with long yellow hair and a pointed face. He wore a dark blue pin-striped double-breasted suit. Despite his height he looked a little like a mouse; at that moment his red, tearful eyes emphasized the resemblance. When his eyes dried, I saw that they were searching, a little furtive. His manner was somehow unsure.

There was a feeling of mutual distrust between us at once. He could not figure out why I was there, and the name Leonid Andreyev meant little to him. He probably saw me as a rival journalist and therefore thought that I was not quite trustworthy. When he heard of the projected trip to the Don, which had not yet been canceled, he became visibly anxious to have himself included in the expedition. I did not like his way of making himself agreeable to Sholokhov, almost to the point of obsequiousness. Obviously, Eugene was an intelligent man, but he lacked *cultura*—as refinement of spirit is now called in the USSR. However, Sholokhov brought up the name of Taras Shevchenko, and Eugene became very excited. It turned out that Shevchenko was his favorite poet. The national Ukrainian poet is a symbol of the fight against oppression. Indeed, if Shevchenko's poems have become somehow dated, his career was unique. He was a serf who, through determination and talent, became a painter. In 1838, when he had already become an accomplished artist in the face of immense obstacles, he was bought out of serfdom by a group of Russian artists and writers. A well-known poet, Vassilij Zhukovsky, organized a raffle and its earnings were used to redeem Shevchenko. I had never seen any art works of Shevchenko's in the original until I visited some Moscow collectors. He had been a faithful recorder of his times—and particularly of the peasant's misery. I discovered that he was also a competent artist, transcending the "genre" painting of that period. His early work especially has a slightly primitive strength. When he gained freedom, Shevchenko turned to poetry as a more direct means of voicing his horror of the situation of the Russian and Ukrainian people and his hope for a revolution. He wrote impassioned poems in Ukrainian and for many years was imprisoned by the Czarist government, which refused to allow him to either paint or write. Judging by his self-portraits, Shevchenko must have looked a little like Sholokhov: bushy mustache, white eyebrows, an intelligent, energetic face.

Eugene thought that Shevchenko was the most inspiring figure in all of literature. Progressively he relaxed, his eyes stopped their searching, and he looked at me more trustingly. When Sholokhov had to make some telephone calls, Eugene took the opportunity to ask me questions about the United States. It was at a time when President Eisenhower was soon expected in the USSR, and interest in America ran high. Eugene wanted to find out about the American standard of living as compared with the Russian, and did not once try to tell me how far ahead of the United States Russia was. He was well informed about specific economic problems. He wanted to know all about American cars—their prices, their durability, the cost of their upkeep. He complained that the Soviet system of gas stations still is lacking in efficiency, a fact which I once experienced on a trip out of town. I had hired a cab which unfortunately did not have enough gas to take me to my destination. It was around noon, and all the widely dispersed gas stations were closed until three for the lunch break. After a frantic circling around town, the driver had to transfer me to another cab. As a reporter, Eugene had to have a car but he found it sometimes a problem: his car had just recently broken down and was undergoing repairs which would take an inordinately long time.

When Sholokhov came back, the conversation turned to the war. Eugene had fought in the same general area where Sholokhov served as a war correspondent. They had memories in common. Sholokhov became engrossed in telling war stories. He told them extraordinarily well, but I cannot recall them with exactness because they merge in my mind with passages from his chronicle of World War II, *They Fought for Their Country*. There is a sameness about the hideous facts of war, spoken or written. I remember being struck with Sholokhov's deep concern, his revulsion against war.

Many war stories and toasts later, Sholokhov and Eugene began singing. Eugene had a pleasant tenor voice; Sholokhov's was muffled, a little broken, but he knew the marvelous words to the old Cossack songs. Song succeeded song late into the night. Eugene's uneasiness had long since disappeared and his eyes were tearful again. These songs about love and war and revolution are full of nostalgia and echo a longing for freedom which is deep in the Russian people, like this one about the Cossack uprising against Peter the Great:

> *A golden trumpet blew*
> *And Stenka Razin cried:*
> *Cossacks, dear Cossacks*
> *Let us fight as one for freedom*
> *Let us fly to freedom like birds!*

6/ The Lane of the Old Stables

No generous deed will be forgotten, Cossack glory will not perish like a speck of gunpowder on a Cossack rifle. A storyteller with a long gray beard but still full of vigor will speak of the Cossacks in sad, powerful words. Their fame will sweep the whole earth, and all those born afterwards will celebrate them.

—NIKOLAI GOGOL, from *Taras Bulba*

As a writer, Sholokhov is not unlike the French naturalists. He strives for objectivity, using concrete details to describe people and events. The direct manner in which he treats sensuous impressions is partly at the root of his reputation for cynicism. Sholokhov's naturalism often disturbs his Russian readers: one cultivated but conservative

Russian gentleman told me that Sholokhov "wrote of people as if they were dogs" because of the attention given to smells. He was alarmed to discover that I admired Sholokhov's writing. In his books, as well as in his conversation, Sholokhov presents things simply as he perceives them, without extraneous commentary, without any attempt to transcend them for the sake of a judgment. He gives us no comfort in the face of death, but he does give us an aching regret for the past.

Sholokhov is a man kept awake at night by haunting war recollections; he is tortured by visions of blood and destruction. The last time I saw him he told me of a terror-filled nightmare he had had the night before, of a duel with a German soldier. Sholokhov was trying to kill the German soldier, who continually escaped him. He tried to shoot him but bullets would not touch the German. He tried to blow him up but the hand grenade wouldn't explode. Finally, striking out with a rusty razor blade, he found that the German's neck was made of rubber, not to be severed no matter how great Sholokhov's effort; soon the razor blade was breaking in his hand.

This last visit with Sholokhov was the one time I saw him alone, and it was shortly before I left Moscow. Because Sholokhov had been ill with the flu, I had not seen him for several weeks. I knew that he had left the Hotel Budapest, but I did not know whether he was still in Moscow. The time of my departure was nearing. Those were hectic days, full of good-byes and last-minute errands and a feeling of mounting sadness. My life in Moscow was so intense that it seemed impossible that it should be arbitrarily interrupted just because I had a plane reservation on a given day of the coming week.

When Sholokhov called me one morning at the Metropole, I broke a previous engagement in order to see him and say good-bye that evening. Sholokhov said that he was now staying in his apartment, in the Arbat, the old section of Moscow. In this neighborhood there are still narrow streets, wooden merchants' houses, and an occasional nineteenth-century mansion surrounded by a garden; these mansions, elegant in their Empire styling, are now government offices.

In English, the name of Sholokhov's street is "lane of the old stables," and I hoped that he might be living in one of those two-story log houses with the carved windows and doors of nineteenth-century Russia. I had never been inside such a house. From the outside they made me think of the house in which Nastasia Filippovna is killed by Rogozhin in *The Idiot;* they seem shut off from the world, with their windows hung in dusty lace, so dark and decayed.

But when, at dusk, I took a taxi to the "lane of the old stables," it turned out that Sholokhov lived in one of a group of modern apartment houses—plain, straight, concrete structures, much like Parisian middle-income developments built in the thirties. They are very comfortable by Moscow standards, and Sholokhov's apartment is on the top floor of one of them, overlooking old Moscow.

When I saw Sholokhov I realized that his sickness had been serious: he was thin and pale and looked older. His face was drawn. But it was good to see him in his home, outside of the impersonal surroundings of the hotel. He somehow looked more relaxed, more likeable than I had ever seen him before.

The apartment was small: three rooms, perhaps four, furnished with absolute simplicity. As I came in I had a glimpse of a medium-sized kitchen with a gas stove, and of a modern bathroom across the hall. In the dining room the table was covered with a red and white oilcloth, and lighted by a low overhanging lamp. There were simple straight chairs and a small couch covered with a hand-crocheted white spread. I could see through a half-open door a bedroom with an old-fashioned narrow iron bed also covered with a white lacy spread. A big desk stood by the window. There were no pictures on the walls, nor were any books in evidence. Sholokhov explained that this apartment was usually occupied by one or the other of his children, now in their twenties, and by his wife when she came to Moscow from Veshenskaia.

Sholokhov's cook had prepared dinner for us. "Something home-made," said Sholokhov. "You must be tired of hotel cooking." It was a dish of cabbage and sausages in the southern Russian style, and indeed it was delicious. We sat down to this informal meal and to a last conversation.

For the first time, Sholokhov spoke a little about his writing, and said how anxious he was to go back to it in the peace of his Don village now that the Supreme Soviet was over. He spoke with nostalgia of his working room, of his desk. "But even there I am too often interrupted. Last year I got some writing done in Kazakhstan—just got away and stayed anonymously in a small village and worked. It was good. Besides my responsibilities as a Deputy, I have a special problem as far as interruptions are concerned. A great many former soldiers write novels and they immediately think of me; they want me to read what they have done and encourage them. Good soldiers are numerous in Russia, but good writers are scarce anywhere. As you perhaps know, we have regional publishing houses in the USSR. The one in the capital of the Don country, in Rostov, receives a great many such novels and it is my responsibility to read some of them."

Sholokhov also spoke with obvious concern about Russian writers who found themselves in exile. In particular he spoke of Kuprin, a follower of Gorki, a very promising realist who wrote, among other things, a rather sensational novel about prostitutes, *Yama*, recently republished in the United States. Like many other émigré writers, Kuprin could not write at all outside of Russia. It was as if Russia was a metaphysical force closely linked to a Russian writer's creativity.

Indeed, it is safe to say that Russia *is* a metaphysical force in the eyes of Sholokhov. This view of Russia is a mystique which has survived in the Communist era—Push-kin, Dostoevsky, Block were filled with it—a kind of na-tionalism strengthened perhaps by sufferings borne in com-mon.

Sholokhov admitted that Ivan Bunin seemed to be an exception to all this. Bunin was less affected by exile than most writers and continued to produce and develop while outside Russia. Kuprin and Bunin were members of the same literary circle, *Znanie*—"knowledge"—named for a publishing house founded by Gorki in 1901. (My grand-father had also belonged to this circle for a while.) Sho-lokhov told me about a short story of Bunin's which he especially admired: On a river boat, a young, cynical officer makes love to a married, slightly melancholy lady passenger traveling alone. He awakens to the cold river morning to find her gone. In the gray light his eyes suddenly fall upon a half-empty glass from which she had drunk the night be-fore, and a hairpin on a table. He is a tough, rough-and-tumble man, something of a cad, but all at once the sight of these humble objects makes him break down. All the repressed tenderness, all the regrets, all the self-pity are suddenly released in a torrent of tears. The glass of water and that hairpin delighted Sholokhov.

Sholokhov and I were still sitting at the table. When he finished recounting the story he asked me to pour out some more tea. It was time for me to go but I didn't want to relinquish the feeling of serenity which Sholokhov imparted; it was almost unique among the Russians I met. He might be tormented by thoughts about war, by other thoughts too, no doubt, but he seemed to me essentially a man who has come to terms with the world. Very few people ever do who also have the strength, or the ruthlessness, to remain faithful to themselves.

As I leaned against the table, the oilcloth, shiny and clean, felt good against my arms. Its contact brought back to my mind half-forgotten evenings in Paris spent at a table covered with a similar oilcloth, with a lamp hanging low overhead, listening to Russian conversation and to the reading of Russian books. Across the table, Sholokhov was thoughtful. He was wearing a heavy white cotton shirt of a very old-fashioned cut. It was strange to feel so at home with somebody belonging to a different milieu, a different generation. Sholokhov is a man of my father's age, a hardened generation in Russia: yet, through him I had come close to understanding a devotion to Russia which was new to me. I knew I was leaving behind something I probably would never again recapture.

THE MUSCOVITES

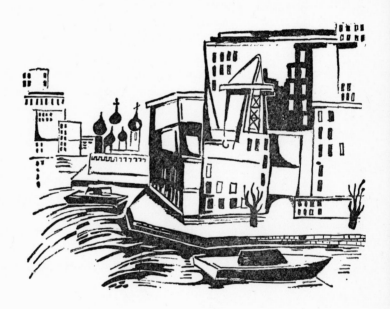

7 / The Tretyakovka

The first part of my stay in Moscow was lovely.
I remember its every detail; for a while, everything around
me appeared picturesque and meaningful. I felt like young
Marcel Proust when he had just arrived in Balbec. For
Proust, life at the seashore contained a thousand promises of
new people and of new landscapes. He had no responsibili-

ties to anyone, his impressions of the resort hadn't become dulled by habit, life was full of freshness and freedom.

For a time, Moscow was like a kind of Balbec to me, a town of discoveries and encounters, yet predictable enough through family tales not to be disturbing despite the new political and social situation with which I was confronted. On first acquaintance, the Russians I met had the charm of characters out of novels who somehow had come to life. Thus my desire to meet Sholokhov was enhanced by my memory of Gogol's Cossacks and the Ukrainian characters in the *Mirgorod* stories.

Except for the fact that I was to bring back some interviews for the *Paris Review* if possible, I was free to do what I liked. I had no close relatives in Moscow other than my young cousin. I could spend my days exactly as I wished; my time was all my own. Unhurriedly, I started an investigation of the Moscow art world. My interview with Ilya Ehrenburg was an incentive in this direction. My main interest was in the literary life, but there was no doubt in my mind that literature and art must have many things in common which would be enlightening.

Meeting people, whether artists or writers, presented no problem. I had many names of friends of my family on whom I might call. Most of them were elderly intellectuals: scholars, men of letters, old-school revolutionaries. At first I wondered whether for their sake, it was prudent to visit them. After all, I came straight from the United States. To my great relief, I discovered that friends had no hesitation in asking me to their homes. Times had changed, intellectuals were no longer under suspicion. A few days before my arrival in Moscow, at a New Year's party at the Kremlin, Khrushchev had pointedly proposed a toast to the intelligentsia, whose very name had been anathema through-out Stalin's regime.

For a while, I led a relaxed existence, enjoying the comforts of the Metropole, where my tourist coupons al-lowed me to have caviar three times a day if I wanted. At night I visited friends of my family. I was usually asked to tea, a light meal which took place in the early evening. It included excellent strong tea (and occasionally very poor coffee), sandwiches, fruit and sweets. Sweets are an impor-tant part of the Russian diet. I had never seen adults eat so many candies and cookies—to combat the effects of the cold, I gather. I too found myself eating them, especially after spending some time out of doors. Tea-drinking, usu-ally with some vodka on the side, was a ritual and there was no possibility of visiting someone without partaking of both. Often, my parents' friends had also invited two or three younger people with literary interests; or else, know-ing that I was a painter, they invited artists. Everyone was very anxious to meet a visitor from the United States. One introduction led to another; in a matter of a few weeks I had a sizable group of acquaintances. I soon became in-volved in my new friends' lives, and I lost the festive free-dom of Proust at Balbec.

During those first weeks in Moscow, I indulged my passion for museum-going. I even did a little sketching out of doors when the wind was not too biting. I loved the snow and the different aspects which it took as light changed throughout the day. I would have liked to paint it although these colors were elusive. Sketching in ink was all I could negotiate. I even had difficulties procuring a draw-ing pad and a bottle of ink: for some reason an art-supply shop was hard to find in Moscow. Finally, I asked a painter friend to get those supplies for me. India ink turned out to be a good medium by which to record the town, the dark figures of people hurrying in the cold and the lacy patterns of small wind-tossed trees growing here and there throughout Moscow.

I did most of my museum-going in the company of one or another of my new friends. Simultaneously, I was learning about their artistic tastes and about Russian art, which I knew only from reproductions. Moscow has a great variety of museums. One painter in love with Russian antiquity consented to escort me only to the Kremlin—other museums didn't interest him. Less single-minded friends agreed to go to the Tretyakov Gallery, or the Tretyakovka, as the Museum of Russian Art is familiarly called in Moscow. But it was the Pushkin Museum, the Moscow Museum of Western Arts which seemed to be the great favorite with Muscovites.

Indeed, the Pushkin is a delightful institution. It is an outstanding museum of fine arts. In a classical nineteenth-century setting it displays works from many collections including the Schukin collection, most of which can be seen at the Hermitage in Leningrad. These paintings are from the nationalized collections of two Russian merchants; thanks to them the USSR possesses a dazzling cross-section of French impressionist art, of Matisses and Picassos. Schukin and Morozov were very much like a certain kind of American collector: coming from a mercantile milieu, without any art training, they appreciated French modern art instinctively long before it was appreciated in France. Schukin in particular had a passion for Matisse and he purchased a number of his works around 1905, at the time of the master's most uninhibited outburst of creativity. The richness of Matisse's designs must have appealed to a Russian's traditional sense of bright decorativeness: at a time when the

Steins were almost alone in recognizing Matisse's genius, Schukin filled his eighteenth-century residence, the Trubetskoy Palace, with dozens of luxurious canvases. Even the most sophisticated art connoisseurs of Russia dismissed Matisse's works then as exclusively decorative.

Today, Muscovites look at those huge, vibrant paintings dreamily, they spend hours on end in front of them, as they do in front of other French canvases. The Monets, the Gauguins, the Van Goghs at the Pushkin Museum are all outstanding. The viewers sometimes look slightly perplexed, but more often than not they are obviously plunged into a state of rapture by the paintings. It is hard to believe that only a few years ago impressionism was considered "decadent" in the USSR.

Victor, a young painter twenty-five years old, offered to accompany me to the Tretyakovka. He was especially intrigued with the evolution of Russian art in the sixteenth and seventeenth centuries and was an habitué of this museum. Friends of my family had taken me to his house one evening shortly after my arrival in Moscow. Victor lived in a relatively comfortable old apartment in the center of town. He shared the apartment with his father and an older brother, a well-known actor in the Moscow legitimate theater. The apartment was full of books. Bookshelves reached from the floor to the ceiling along every wall, while paintings and drawings in portfolios were stacked in the corners.

Victor's painting looked like a promising student's work. He had left the Moscow Art Institute several years before without graduating and earned his living designing art books. He painted on the side. Since commercial art work is well paid in the USSR, Victor could paint for months on end: three books kept him going comfortably for a year or more. He had foregone the advantages offered to members of the Artists' Union—studios, commissions and pensions—but he had retained his independence. At present, artists such as Victor are free to paint pictures in any style and sell them privately. The necessity of conforming to the State's art philosophy concerns only the members of the Artists' Union who are State functionaries. And even for those artists, I was to find out that conformity affects them to varying degrees. Those differences depend on many imponderable factors: an artist's single-mindedness, his self-assurance as an artist, his understanding of when to compromise and when to persevere in his convictions. Overall, the Artists' Union appeared to be a tough, reactionary institution, more narrow-minded than the Writers' Union, perhaps because absurd theories are as a rule easier to promulgate in art than in literature; it is harder to detect faking in the visual arts than in writing.

Victor's works showed that he was influenced by icons, and also by the French painter Georges Rouault, although his subject matter was not religious: he painted portraits and still lifes in vivid colors. The influence of Rouault came from a few reproductions that Victor had collected. There is only one original Rouault to be seen in Moscow, a big water color at the Pushkin Museum.

Visits to the Tretyakovka helped me realize that in order to understand something of Russian art, I would have to suppress for a while a painter's attitude towards painting —the perpetual probing of what is esthetically successful, or unsuccessful, and why. Russian painting, with the exception of the icons, has primarily a historical interest.

The Tretyakovka is a weighty monument to the seriousness with which Russians regarded—and still regard—painting and sculpture. It is a spreading, nineteenth-century structure, built in an ornate imitation of a Russian traditional style, with crenelated walls, mosaics, and turrets. From the outside, it intimates that one will be soon confronted with something ponderous and very Russian. Many painters whose works are shown at the Tretyakovka were talented, all were conscientious, they were accomplished draftsmen but they were hopelessly hampered by the academism of their conceptions. Often their drawings are marvelous, full of life, but when those drawings are painstakingly translated into vast, contrived compositions, they lose all their charm. The Russians never resolved the problem which the impressionists tackled as they went to paint outdoors in their straw hats. The Russians stayed in their studios pondering all sorts of complicated, artificial situations. They failed to establish a subjective contact with the visual world, a contact which was the impressionists' lasting contribution to painting and is an essential condition of "realism," to give this term its most general meaning, that of art trying to seize the ever changing tangible world. There were Russian realists, of course, who didn't allow their inspiration to be hampered by misleading Victorian art theories and have left us some beautiful paintings.

Victor knew the history of Russian art intimately. He led me at once to the outstanding paintings at the Tretyakovka. Thus I saw the lovely portraits by A. Venezianov suffused with a golden light, of peasant girls in immobile poses, with their red bonnets, round and flat, not unlike the Florentine hats whose geometric shapes had fascinated Pablo Ucello. We admired the landscapes by Isaac Levithan, who had understood the lessons of impressionism and applied them to the Russian countryside with a personal softness. Then Victor showed me the works of A. M. Vrubel who had had considerable fame in his day. Boris Pasternak describes in his autobiography how as a very small child filled with awe he visited Vrubel's studio with his father and saw a painting entitled *The Demon*, which Vrubel had just finished. *The Demon*, inspired by Lermontov's poem, now hangs at the Tretyakovka. It is a symbolic painting which has no power to move us today. Yet Vrubel had great talent. He made many superb Cézannesque pencil portraits of his contemporaries.

Victor pointed out to me several airy oil portraits by Valentin Serov—his more ambitious compositions are quite dull, although he is regarded in Russia as a master. All of a sudden, we saw a portrait of Leonid Andreyev by Serov. It was hanging high in a room of nineteenth-century paintings, above two or three rows of pictures. My grandfather was seen in profile, he was seated on the grass, wearing a Russian shirt of white embroidered linen set off by a background of summery bright green. Painted sketchily, it was a figure full of a strange liveliness, which was heightened by the dullness of the maroon wall against which it hung. The Victorian approach to art exhibiting—pictures all over the wall on top of each other, dark walls, hangings of burgundy colored velvet—is the only one known at the Tretyakovka.

Most of the paintings at the Tretyakovka had an anecdotal interest; they were an excellent illustration of the Russian past and often had a quaint charm. Always they testified to the excellence of their author's intentions—how many canvases are displayed showing the fate of the Russian peasant in the nineteenth century! It is easy to believe that those works helped in the fight against oppression, but as works of art they remain derivative and sentimental.

They lack spontaneity and that intangible all-important element, plastic sense. After a few days in Moscow, I couldn't help feeling that this lack of plastic sense was perhaps partly due to northern light. Unlike Mediterranean light which breaks objects into planes, Russian light softens contours; it creates a vague misty atmosphere which speaks to the mind rather than to the senses.

Victor and I discussed endlessly the future of Russian art as we went from one crowded room of nineteenth-century art to another. The Tretyakovka was always teeming with people: young and old, peasants, workers, students; attentive, eager faces were to be seen everywhere. Victor made commendable efforts at pointing out to me the works of interest in a sea of second-rate pictures.

Suddenly he looked at his watch and said with a conspiratorial air, "Let's go to the icon rooms now. The Museum will be closing in less than an hour. Let's look at some real painting. We have given our due to the Academy . . ."

He led me through the whole length of the immense Tretyakovka. We crossed halls of recent, gray-looking official paintings, samples of what the Russians call the "jacket school of painting" because it depicts Lenin and Stalin in historical situations invariably clad in gray or khaki jackets. At the very end of the building we reached a couple of isolated small rooms. Their walls were covered with magnificent icons. How luminous, how strong they looked! I was excited and moved—by the icons, and by Victor's fierce love of them. He was familiar with every one on display. There were about a hundred to be seen, among them the famous *Three Angels of Abraham* by Andrei Rublev. "This is only about a hundredth of the Tretyakovka's collection of icons," Victor said. The daylight was fading and the museum's closing time was nearing, but the rooms were still full of silent people intently looking at the pictures. The icons, painted in transparent, glowing tones, could be seen clearly despite the oncoming darkness. Victor led me from one to another, telling me what he knew about the history of each. "Do you realize that Matisse wept with excitement when he first came into this room during a visit to Moscow in the thirties?" he said. It delighted him to be able to show me something completely Russian which could be admired wholeheartedly. Slim and dark, with an elongated face and fine eyebrows, he himself looked like one of the saints on the icons. With his thin hands, lovingly he outlined for me the intricacies of the *Three Angels*, known also as Rublev's *Trinity*, whose theological meaning is complex and which is truly one of the most beautiful medieval paintings in existence. Then we looked at Rublev's saints. Victor was a little embarrassed because they had acquired lay names on the descriptive labels—St. Michael and St. George had become Michael and George. The icons, even more than in the Kremlin where the icons are incorporated into large altars, revealed an astonishing variety of subjects and forms, yet they bore the marks of a unique vision.

As if the lyric moments spent in the icon rooms called for some kind of unpleasant compensation, it was on that same day that I came across my first instance of Russian rudeness. Leaving the museum at dusk, Victor and I hailed a taxi driving by on a side street. At its wheel was a woman, an enormous mannish creature wearing a hat with earflaps; her unkempt fingernails were painted bright red and a cigarette was hanging from her mouth. I noticed how unattractive she looked—she must have disliked our appearance as well. We were going to have tea at the Metropole and Victor gave its address to the woman. We went on talking as she drove through darkening deep blue Moscow. When we reached the hotel, Victor handed her a ten-ruble bill. With startling unexpectedness, the woman began screaming at us. Having hastily gathered the change she owed Victor, she threw it in his face. She went on and on, using vile language, refusing the tip that Victor hadn't even had time to offer her. She shouted in a voice trembling with rage: "We here in Russia do not need your dirty foreign money!" Victor calmly picked up his coins but as he helped me out of the taxi, I could feel his hand shaking: "These things happen from time to time. Don't get upset," he said, trying to keep his voice detached. "You must understand that for years and years a hatred of intellectuals was inculcated in our people. And she was irritated by the fact that we were going to a hotel where foreigners reside. Hatred of intellectuals and hatred of foreigners go hand in hand . . ."

I must have looked very unhappy because Victor continued, "For heaven's sake don't take this incident personally. I have to be philosophical about this: I have a gift for unleashing the fiendish disposition of this kind of woman. I look absent-minded and gentle, in me they sense an easy prey . . ."

We drank our tea and he told me of an incident which had happened to him shortly before. After a play, he had taken a girl friend to the restaurant on the top floor of the Ukraine Hotel. The Ukraine is a skyscraper with several modern shops and restaurants. The hotel regulations allow customers into the restaurant till twelve-thirty at night. Victor and his friend took a walk after leaving the theater; they got to the Ukraine at ten past twelve. For no accountable reason, the elevator operator, a skinny, nondescript woman in her forties, refused to take them up to the restaurant. Victor went to the hotel desk and complained to the administrator, another woman in her forties, who said rather meekly that indeed Victor and his companion should be admitted to the restaurant since it wasn't twelve-thirty yet. However, she herself seemed a little afraid of the elevator operator. Suddenly, when Victor got back into the elevator the woman operator went into hysterics. She started to yell, accusing both the hotel administrator and poor Victor of being "hooligans." * She continued to yell uncontrollably, and before Victor knew it, it was twelve-thirty and the restaurant had actually closed its doors. Victor, shaken and humiliated, had to take his date home hungry. In wintertime, nothing at all is open in Moscow after twelve-thirty.

"Such women fill similar positions all over," Victor said. "Many of them are widows—there is a terrific gap in our male population as a result of the war. They are frustrated, and once in a while they let themselves go. Intellectuals, an object of hatred and ridicule for so long, are their ready victims. They have discovered too that we rarely answer them back . . ."

* Hooligan means "rascal" in Russian, but it has acquired a particularly pejorative meaning designating the "black jacket" types who defy both the Soviet law and the Soviet sense of respectability.

8 / The Young Men of Moscow

When I am asked my opinion about national-ism, I always answer that I am a nationalist. I think that there are only two nationalities—good people and bad people. And I am for the good ones. Good people sounds like a childish definition, but children are very wise—because they do not try consciously to be wise.

You are Americans. We are Russians. But good Americans will always be closer to me than bad Russians, and to you I am sure good Russians are preferable to bad Americans.

We know very little about you, shockingly lit-tle, but we try to follow certain of your move-ments. . . .

We want to meet you as often as possible, to be able to speak to each other with absolute sincerity. It should help all of us to resolve both our own inner problems and those of the world. You are responsible for the U.S.A., we for Russia but we all live on the same dear earth and we answer for her all together.

—EUGENE EVTUSHENKO, from a letter, 1960

A day will come:
Burning with shame
Our sons will remember
Those strange days
When common honesty was called
Courage . . .

—EUGENE EVTUSHENKO, "A Talk," 1961

From the first day, I was impressed with the vitality of Moscow daily life. Restaurants were always full, museums and theaters were overflowing with people. Theater tickets were hard to procure: fortunately the Intourist office makes it possible for foreigners to obtain them with relative ease. Muscovites were busy with a thousand projects; as if in a great outburst of new-found initiative and energy, people were hurrying to concerts, to art shows, to poetry readings.

I met one of Moscow's most active young men soon after my arrival. Eugene Evtushenko is well known in the Soviet Union and has even earned some fame in the West through a widely publicized poem, "Babii Yar," which attacks anti-Semitism; it originally appeared in the *Literary Gazette*, the organ of the Soviet Writers' Union. This poem, published in 1961 on the eve of Yom Kippur, is full of emotional intensity. It commemorates the German massacres in Kiev: in 1941 approximately forty thousand Jews were murdered in a ravine called "Babii Yar." The poem denounces anti-Semitism in general and the crude, drunken anti-Semitism of certain backward Russians in particular. This same prejudice fanned by the Czarist government caused the widely spread pogroms of the prerevolutionary era. A latent anti-Semitism still exists among certain pseudo-patriotic Russians.

"Babii Yar" was violently criticized in some Soviet circles because the existence of anti-Semitism is not acknowledged in the USSR; indeed, racism is declared to be incompatible with Communist ideals. A literary journal, *Literature and Life*, denounced Evtushenko for ignoring the

Communist Party's official opposition to anti-Semitism. It even labeled him a "pigmy cosmopolitan" in the best tradition of Soviet name calling.

Some commentators took those facts to signify that Evtushenko was ostracized. For instance, *Paris Match* introduced him to its readers as the "poète maudit de la Place Rouge" in an article full of outrageously inaccurate information. It really signified that a certain amount of give and take has appeared within the Writers' Union and in Soviet publications in recent years. Ehrenburg's *People, Life, Years* may be bitterly attacked for its "cosmopolitanism" and still go on being serialized in *Novii Mir;* Evtushenko's love poems have often been termed "indecent" and "decadent" but still are being printed and read; the well-known writer Konstantin Paustovsky openly attended Pasternak's funeral without suffering personally or professionally in any way; the Soviet Secretary to Cultural Affairs, Ekaterina Furtseva, was criticized for the inadequate output of the Soviet playwrights without public rebuke, and so on. Needless to say, this does not mean that Soviet literary life has become free. Simply, Russian leaders have realized that a certain amount of controversy is not incompatible with the good functioning of the Soviet State, that it even has beneficent effects on public life. Within the frame of Communist thinking, one of the oldest Russian disputes has revived, that which opposes "patriots" to "universalists." Like Dostoevsky, Sholokhov is a patriot, while Ehrenburg is a universalist, as Turgenev was. By their very nature, the patriots' convictions often lead to chauvinism and even to fanaticism. As for the universalists, they are accused of being slavish admirers of everything foreign. Clearly, the USSR has suffered from excesses of patriotism in recent years. The fact that the universalists' point of view is now upheld in the USSR is in itself a gratifying innovation. *

Implicitly, young Evtushenko has adopted the universalists' stand despite a working-class Russian background; his origins give greater impact to his voice. In spite of a reprimand for slandering his compatriots in "Babii Yar," his popularity in Russia has steadily increased. Of course, Evtushenko's personality and his career are as much a product of new forces within Russia as he is a force in himself, an "engineer of human souls" as writers are pompously but aptly called by the Soviet Communist Party. Evtushenko cannot be defined easily; he is neither a "beatnik" nor a "*poète maudit*" nor a "pure poet" nor a "politician." It might be argued that he has a touch of all of these types, but let us emphasize first that he is both a convinced Communist and a good poet. He is an influential member of the literary section of the Moscow Komsomol (the rumor that he was at one time expelled from the Komsomol is without foundation). Better than anyone else right now, he dramatically unites those contradictory and ever-present elements in the best of Russian writers, patriotism and a longing for universality: both stem from an exalted feeling of a writer's responsibility to his readers.

* Ilya Ehrenburg has written the following for instance: "The eighteenth-century satirists made fun of Russian noblemen who tried to be like the French. I dislike the Soviet philistine who on seeing some vulgar American film says to his wife: We have a long way to go! I am however willing to make a very low bow not only to Shakespeare or to Cervantes but also to Chaplin and Hemingway, and I do not think that it could possibly degrade me. Endless talk about one's superiority is bound up with servility towards everything foreign— those are the various aspects of the same old inferiority complex and I dislike just as much the other type of philistine who reviles, be it sincerely or hypocritically, everything good if it is foreign." (From an instalment of Ehrenburg's memoirs published in *Novii Mir* in the summer of 1961.)

Evtushenko came to see me at the Metropole one dark snowy afternoon in January. My father had met him once at Boris Pasternak's in 1957, and had liked him. Before I left Geneva, he suggested that I call Evtushenko while I was in Moscow; the young poet had promised my father a book of his poems but was unable to give it to him at the time because the book was out of print. Three years later, the book was still unavailable, but Evtushenko accepted my invitation to tea. It was one of those muffled days when to stay indoors and drink tea and converse is a special pleasure. The snowfall was heavy and it obscured the daylight: lamps were turned on in my room, where we were served tea and raspberry jam.

Very tall and slender, with transparent blue eyes, Evtushenko was wearing a hat of pale gray astrakhan which was extremely becoming to him. He is fair and has high cheekbones, his eyes are narrow and shrewd. His manner had a kind of winning candidness, yet it seemed a little calculated, as that of a flirtatious child. One recognized at once a young man who has risen in the world through talent and wits and has come to rely on the fact that his wits are appreciably superior to those of almost everyone else. There was a certain flamboyance to Evtushenko's manner and he played the classic role of a romantic young poet with gusto. I knew that Evtushenko was immensely popular with Soviet youth. His popularity is comparable to that of a movie star in the West.

His flamboyance didn't prevent Evtushenko from being an attentive conversationalist. He was anxious to tell me about Moscow literary life; he guessed at once what would interest and touch me, perhaps because we belong approximately to the same generation. Our conversation, which lasted into mid-evening, was punctuated with stanzas from his poems. Evtushenko recites poetry with extraordinary effectiveness. Among other poems he quoted those of Leonid Martinov, one of the best Soviet poets of my father's generation. Martinov has a certain lyric informality which must have influenced Evtushenko in his beginnings as a poet. As happens in certain encounters when people come across the same preoccupations at once, everything that Evtushenko said and recited that afternoon was like an answer to questions that I hadn't had time yet to formulate. It was as if Evtushenko had sensed that he could answer some of the questions that were on my mind, and one in particular: what are young Russians like? Not in the dull statistical sense, but in fact, as human beings.

Evtushenko was in a position to introduce me to his contemporaries, to interpret their spirit for me and in this respect he proved an invaluable and brave friend.

During that first afternoon Evtushenko told me about his childhood and he asked about mine—what I said about spending the war years on Ile d'Oléron, a small island in the Atlantic, aroused his curiosity. He was intrigued with the idea of a Russian family living in this remote part of France. He told me that he was from a modest family in a Siberian village. During the war, his family was dispersed and he himself was too young to fight. He came to Moscow and, as he put it, "slept under a staircase and lived almost exclusively on sorrel leaves." His first poems, published when he was sixteen years old, were an immediate success.

Indeed, Evtushenko's career has depended partly on his remarkable facility as a poet. He said that he was able to go to the *Literary Gazette*'s offices—he contributes regularly to this newspaper—and write a poem on a given theme in a few hours. Thus his poems are uneven, sometimes brash, with a journalistic stamp on them, but they are always individual. Evtushenko has a certain tone all his own. At best, his poems are tender, yet virile. He is frequently compared to Mayakovsky, and his mixture of declarative matter-of-factness and subjectivity is reminiscent of that great revolutionary poet. Evtushenko is, of course, a lesser poet than Mayakovsky, but as an individual he too has created an image of the poet as a Communist participating in public affairs. Paradoxically, in a society in which all poets have been expected to voice their adherence to Communist ideals and to participate in politics, those two almost alone have created such a public image. Every other outstanding Russian poet of our time—Akhmatova, Mandelstam, Martinov —emphasizes the individual rather than the social role of man.

In fact, Evtushenko's tone as a poet is deceptively simple and it is misleading to compare him to some other poet. Without being a poetic genius, he has created a lyric style which is the mark of a generation in the USSR. He has asserted and sung his own spontaneity, his optimism, his youth. Youth proved a powerful force against the monolithic official ways.

Youth is Evtushenko's principal theme, or rather his consistent point of view. From this point of view, an uninhibited young revolutionary poet can look at Soviet reality with enthusiasm, but also with indignation when this reality in which he feels responsible is disappointing. Evtushenko's poems are often invectives despite their disarming exterior: they are directed against hypocrisy, they clamor for more love, more intelligence, more imagination . . .

That afternoon Evtushenko asked many questions about beatnik writing: he had read *On the Road*, which had just been translated into Russian then. This interest was not accidental. Although technically he is an accomplished poet, which cannot be said of our beatniks, Evtushenko shares with them a certain similarity of approach. The accidental quality of abstract expressionist painting, the stream of consciousness in beatnik poetry as well as the social protest it embodies, are marks of many artists now thirty years old. Evtushenko, who can be a profound poet and is always skillful, does have a gift for capturing an object or a situation freshly which is vaguely akin to beatnik poets' attempts at directness. Evtushenko also has a keen if not infallible sense of what is contemporary in form. This in itself sets him aside from most other Soviet writers who are content as a rule to follow established formal patterns in their works.

As we drank endless glasses of tea during that long afternoon and I listened to him, fascinated by his dash and his perspicacity, Evtushenko told me how the first outdoor public poetry reading, now a yearly event in Moscow, had taken place in 1955. In October of that year, a group of young poets organized a sale of inscribed books at one of Moscow's larger bookstores. Spontaneously a crowd gathered. Before long, several hundred people stood outside the store. On the spur of the moment and despite the cold weather, the poets carried makeshift tables out of doors and sold their books to "a thousand hands" as Evtushenko described it. When their books were sold out, the poets climbed in turn on the tables and read their poems. Evening neared and snowflakes began to fall but for hours the crowd stood in the street and listened. Since then, an afternoon of public reading and of selling books has become a tradition in Moscow in the fall—and a symbol of new times.*

* The 1961 poetry reading was the occasion of a great personal triumph for Eugene Evtushenko. It took place shortly after the "Babii Yar" controversy and Evtushenko was not among the poets on the official tribune. However, when it was somehow found out that he was in the audience, he was given a triumphal ovation and forced to recite his poems standing by Mayakovsky's oversized statue.

Then Evtushenko spoke of the birth of a new intelligentsia in the USSR. "It is like trying to catch a flow of water in the palm of your hand," he said. "Most of it flows out but a little is retained in the cup of the hand. This is happening now. We and our children will eventually retain this little amount of water as against the main stream—but of course the ever increasing main stream is our first concern. The fact that the Soviet government has been able to open the world of good books to the masses of people gives us faith in the future of Russia." In his words, I could detect an unconscious longing to capture the spirit of the old intelligentsia about which he was curious and for which he professed the greatest respect.

"A new public is growing up in Russia," he continued. "One about to become more sophisticated than the writers themselves. Our writers are faced with an immense task. Our poetry is full of life, and the great tradition of the twenties—of Mayakovsky and Essenin—has been at least partially preserved. Prose has not so far been equal to poetry: poetry, the art of the heart, withstood adversity best. Yet just think of all the subject matter not touched upon in prose. Think of the thirties, how much there is to tell . . ." He spoke about the short-story writer Yuri Kazakov whose books he promised to bring me. I recognized the name of an author whom Ehrenburg had mentioned as being one of the most talented young writers working at present in the USSR.

I asked Evtushenko why contemporary books of poetry were so difficult to come by in Moscow. One has to hunt for them, stand in line, ask friends to procure them. "The printings are not small," he said. "Twenty thousand copies in the case of my last book. But it is inadequate, considering that poetry is our leading art form . . ." and indeed in the company of my young cousin I had attended a couple of electrifying poetry readings, overflowing with listeners of all ages and all social backgrounds. I had heard poetry recited everywhere I went, not only by poets or students, but also by simple people, who quoted Pushkin and Mayakovsky. The poetic references were sometimes a little shaky, but this sometimes gave them a charm of their own.

As for the intellectuals, they read Mandelstam and Pasternak and a score of new and often excellent poets, some of whom were not published. The new poetry is often modern in form, reminiscent of the French surrealist poet Henri Michaux. This flourishing of poetry was a source of delight to me. It was strange and wonderful to find that poetry could in our own time have a vast appeal. I asked Evtushenko about the publishing of poetry. "When a young poet presents his verse to a publishing house or a magazine, it is carefully reviewed," he said. "Parts or all of it used to be rejected on the grounds of being too exclusively lyrical, too formal, too ambiguous. Great progress has been made in recent years, however. Poetry is nowadays more often judged on its merits rather than on its content. Lyric poetry has gained official recognition. But there are some awfully reactionary types among our officials still. It is our responsibility —mine and that of other younger writers—to improve our publishing. Not that our responsibility stops at publishing. We feel that the future is in our hands—a fabulous future, which is there to blossom. We are at a crucial time of our history, we just cannot afford to be selfish. Now or never is the time to bring forth the best in our country. Olga Vadimovna, there is so much which is good in Moscow now—in poetry, in painting—and in people . . ."

I asked Evtushenko if poets could make their living with their poetry. He pointed out to me how highly regarded writers were in the USSR. "This is an old Russian tradition; reading is our national pastime. Public readings or an occasional movie script supplement the income poets derive from the publishing of their poems. Traveling is made easy for us since it is supposed to benefit our inspiration . . ."

Evtushenko seemed to know everyone in Moscow. Through him, I met a number of young people who were like himself active members of the Writers' Union, or Artists' Union in the case of artists and sculptors. They believed in the greatness of Russian destiny, they felt they were on the threshold of a new era and of a new art. They filled me with astonishment and with some envy: this enthusiasm was so unlike the atmosphere in the West. And those young artists and writers who were not members of official organizations and led more private and contemplative lives were equally eager to read or show their works and to discuss with passion the future of the USSR and of the world.

Evtushenko was usually very busy with his affairs, but once in a while we spent an evening together. He would take me to a poetry reading, to a painter's studio or a movie screening. I saw Chekhov's *Lady with a Little Dog* in his company. I was enchanted with this film while Evtushenko, an uncompromising champion of modern art, found it a little old-fashioned. (Incidentally, when this movie reached France, the painter Marc Chagall, who reportedly saw it five times, said: "It is an amazing movie. How is it that a young Soviet movie director was able to re-create old Russia with such precision, such tact, such delicacy—such love? The young people are somehow able to go back to the authentic origins of Russian national art . . .")

One day, we went to the studio of the painter Yuri Vassiliev, a versatile artist who was then experimenting with various forms of surrealism. I wasn't too taken by Vassiliev's paintings but Evtushenko, a close friend of Vassiliev, admired them. I preferred Vassiliev's sculptures, while Evtushenko liked the pictures full of rotating spheres, spaceships of the future, and sputniks. I had a running argument about art with Evtushenko. He considered me too conservative because of my preference for nature as a subject matter. I assured him that he lacked insight into the problems of painting, that he was too intellectual in his approach. His literary taste was informed and quite original (although he did say that *Doctor Zhivago* smelled of mothballs), but his preferences in painting suffered from lack of background in modern art, as is so often the case with young Russians. However, he was intensely interested in painting in that peculiar Russian fashion which considers painting as an extension of literature rather than a world of its own.

Evtushenko's life seemed to be a constant, exciting probing of himself and his surroundings. He could be charming, and humorous. He was generous. I owe him a small library of recent Russian verse which he gave me to take back with me. This included a volume of his *Collected Verse*, which he assured me he had had to steal from his mother's library, to send to my father. Books of poetry were invaluable presents. Once a book of poetry is out of print—and printings of twenty to a hundred thousand are reported to sell out in half a day—it is usually unavailable for a long time. It becomes a rare, coveted possession. I had the suspicion—confirmed by what Sholokhov had once said of whole printings by uninteresting but influential authors being sent directly from the storerooms to paper mills—that Soviet publishing operates on a principle of equality rather than of supply and demand: all poets of the Union have to have their books printed whether their poems are read or not. This and the fact that certain poets, considered to be "too far out," are not published at all explains the lively traffic of type-written poetry between friends.

I was forever surprised at the seriousness behind Evtushenko's dash. "You have come to see us at a good moment," he said once, alluding to the fact that several measures were recently passed in the Supreme Soviet concerning the undue privileges of Soviet high functionaries. Salaries had been cut down and the use of chauffeured cars was canceled for certain officials. Evtushenko took the fight against those officials, known as the "Drozdovs," to heart —as have all the best Soviet writers. Drozdov is a character in Vladimir Dudintzev's novel *Not By Bread Alone,* and Drozdov has come to stand for a high functionary who is cynical, backward, opportunistic, powerful and usually a former Stalinist.* "In this fight against deadliness, we must join forces," said Evtushenko. And it was true that the young poets and painters whom I met—and all were active in their respective Unions—shared a similar feeling of dedication. There was less back-biting than is usual in small tightly knit groups, or so it seemed to me. I can only speak for the young men I personally came to know, but it was striking because in general Muscovites seemed to have more than their share of squabbles. Russians do not hide their emotions, and intricate, stormy relationships between friends are the rule.

---

* A courageous speech by Konstantin Paustovsky denounced the "Drozdovs" as early as 1956. Here is his definition of the "Drozdovs": "This is a new group of acquisitive carnivores, a group which has nothing in common with the Revolution, or with our regime, or with socialism. They are cynics, black obscurantists . . . who quite openly carry on anti-Semitic talk of a kind worthy of pogrom-makers.

There are thousands of these Drozdovs and we should not close our eyes to their existence . . . we cannot at any price close our eyes, unless we are willing to allow these Drozdovs to overrun our entire country." (As quoted in *Year of Protest,* 1956)

Two of Evtushenko's friends are at present considered to be the most promising young artists in Moscow. They are the poet Andrei Voznesenski and the sculptor Ernst Neizvestni. Andrei Voznesenski's popularity among young Russians is second only to Evtushenko's, while he often ranks first with connoisseurs. His verse is full of youthfulness and talent—youth is his main theme as it is Evtushenko's; in Voznesenski, however, it is never coquettish. Technically Voznesenski has learned from Pasternak and Tsvetayeva, but he has a completely personal sense of both rhythm and visual imagery; he loves and understands painting and finds inspiration in Rubens, Renoir and Goya. He was trained as an architect and has been publishing his poems only for the past three years, but his rise was meteoric.

He is a compelling, very young man with a childlike face and blue eyes. Slight, quick, he wears a snap-brim cap and looks like a student. Besides his outstanding poetic powers, he has a light-heartedness both as a person and as a poet which is characteristic of the new Soviet generation. His amused and tender love for the Russian way of life, for both its good and less good aspects, is in contrast with the high-mindedness of a Pasternak or a Tsvetayeva. Thus Voznesenski compares a bunch of lilac carried by someone on a crowded train to a poodle who jumps and nuzzles; in another poem, a woman cashier—symbol of an inefficient, tyrannic routine—"rises like dough in her formidable anger."

The sculptor Ernst Neizvestni is in his late thirties, and belongs to a generation which was directly affected by war. Those who fought in it as very young men have hardened and matured early. Ernst was a "desentchnik"—a man who is sent behind enemy lines to do underground fighting.

This is a form of combat which was considered most dangerous, and he earned many decorations in the war. As an artist, he is an exciting and rare phenomenon: he is a good artist who is to a considerable extent adapted to the special circumstances in which he works. He works "functionally" and yet with sincerity. In his case, the function of art is primarily architectural.

Ernst stresses that above all he doesn't want to be a "misunderstood artist," a role for which he feels temperamentally unsuited. He carves his large statues in an expressionistic style which unites successfully his own view of art with the realism favored by his patron, the State. He also does bronzes which he sells to friends and to private collectors, who are numerous in Moscow. Those smaller works are all on the subject of war. In spirit they remind one of Kathe Kollowitz but they have an angular style to them: torn, dismembered, barely recognizable victims of violence are treated both realistically and yet in a completely modern manner. Those compositions are sought after by Moscow art lovers.

Ernst is an intense person, of uncommon vitality, massive, with curly graying hair and coal black eyes. He is always dressed in shabby working clothes. A passionate patriot, he wants to create an art which speaks to every Russian heart, and which will do honor to his country. He considers it his responsibility to try to improve the Russian official taste and he works at it within the Artists' Union. "If the Soviet art school has its contradictions and its inconsistencies," Ernst once wrote in a letter, "they are the signs of our growth. Those contradictions are taken up in discussions, in controversies, both oral and in print. I take part in those discussions and have a clearly defined position, a progressive one. My point of view is sustained by the sharper, stronger works of older Soviet artists . . ." Because of his exceptional resilience and conviction he is able to resolve to his own satisfaction the differences between his tastes and the requirements of the projects on which he works; and he knows that only the State can provide him with the vast projects for which his talent is best suited. He has an innate feeling for material—stone, cement, iron; this appeals to many Soviet architects who at this time lean toward a more functional, modern style of architecture. Ernst's talent is attuned to the large edifices which are now under construction—stadiums, theaters, youth centers . . . His sense of the monumental echoes the contemporary mood in the Soviet Union, but his work, inspired by the universal theme of physical suffering, has an impact which exceeds that of most Soviet art.

At the time of my first visit to Ernst's studio, he occupied a small cramped room in the basement of a government office building; it was an art publishing house, I believe. This studio proved nearly impossible to locate. Evtushenko had given me its address, but it turned out to be in an area of construction and the new street had not yet been completed and there were no signs. One morning I searched interminably among blocks of modern office buildings and adjacent small wooden houses. Nearby, along the main avenue leading out of town, an open market looked like a scene from an older Moscow, full of people in country clothes, noisy, wrapped up in their trading and shopping. The modern buildings, half finished and unmarked, looked forlorn. I had all but given up finding Neizvestni when a helpful *baba* selling candy from a makeshift stall explained the situation to me and eventually I found the sculptor's small basement.

I will always remember the excitement of my first moments there. Perhaps I was even more impressed because this visit took place after seeing the work of some young artists who painted weak imitations of Western styles based on postcard reproductions and newspaper clippings; I also had seen some boring but ambitious efforts by artists belonging to the Union who seemed unable to shift successfully from often brilliant studies to the larger compositions which are expected of a painter in the USSR.

But in this basement realistic works suddenly took on life. There were black-brown studies of heads in cast iron, an oversized young mother of granite, a dying man in bronze . . . These works, huge and rough-looking, had something of the breadth of the art of Mexico in the twenties and thirties. It was as if Orozco's figures had acquired a third dimension. Yet those sculptures had a completely Russian look. One might be at a loss to define precisely what a "Russian look" is in sculpture except perhaps by comparing an Aztec face to a Russian one. Instead of polished, angular features, the Russian face is round with heavy cheekbones and arched eyebrows, a big nose: "A nose like a potato," is a common Russian phrase.

Ernst, who looked like one of his own statues, unbelievably solid, showed me some beautiful drawings for an immense war memorial he was working on. We talked for a long time about war and art. He was intelligent and imaginative and he seemed anxious to tell me about his life as a Soviet artist. He united patriotism with open-mindedness. Ernst's conversation echoed certain deeply felt preoccupations in the Soviet Union concerning war and oppression and also the necessity to create in the USSR an art fit for a great modern nation. Because of the scope of his talent, he can conquer many problems that would defeat a lesser artist. Ernst is unquestionably one of the most interesting artists now working in the USSR.

As I came to know people like Ernst Neizvestni, I was

impressed with the virility that Russian artistic life possesses. Its very lack of freedom, so distressing to a Westerner, has stimulated those younger people who are particularly strong and daring. Among them, masculine virtues are exalted: creativity, courage, single-mindedness. There is no doubt that the lack of comforts in Soviet daily life is abysmal by American standards—only certain highly placed persons like Sholokhov, for example, enjoy a measure of luxury. But this life has created an exciting challenge for many younger Russians. And in the way they are meeting it lies one of the sources of strength of present-day Russia.

9/ The Old and the New

"*The arguments of freedom shall not die:*
The Roman senate testifies to this . . ."
Lighting his clumsy pipe, he wraps his robe
About him, while the men continue playing chess.

He has exchanged his proud bedeviled dream
For a clearing in Siberia—deaf, lost—
And for this curved chibuk *in his bitter lips*
Which truth, in a world of sadness, dared to cross.

Remember when the German oaks first rustled
And Europe wept, wept in their spreading shade?
Black carriages with four wild horses reared
On each triumphant turn the procession made.

There was a time when blue punch flamed our
        glasses,
With wide and gracious sound the samovar
And the friend across the Rhine of freedom
And romance spoke softly. Ah, deceptive harp!

And the live voices still are agitating
For the fine liberty of citizenship,
But blind skies do not demand their martyrs now—
Toil, constancy, a surer harvest reaps.

The flame is dying fast, the night grows cold,
Reason and right have shifted, gone awry,
And it is sweet to whisper to oneself:
Russia, Lethe, Lorelei.

—OSIP MANDELSTAM, "The Decembrist," 1917,
from *Tristia*

From the beginning I was struck by the fact that Muscovites seemed divided into two groups, the old and the young, as if those over forty had suffered so much that they were unable to come to terms with life again. I am not speaking now of the particularly talented, vital people who have an intense professional life, such as the critic and children's writer Kornei Tchukovsky. Tchukovsky lives in Peredelkino outside of Moscow, where he runs a children's library for the town's children. Now in his eighties, he is one of Russia's most active literary critics. Tchukovsky, Ehrenburg, Paustovsky—those are the exceptions, people with a following among the young. But the usual contrast between young and old distressed me. It was as if the country was divided spiritually into two separate communities. I often thought of my cousin's observation about fear, and I was continually reminded of what many older people had gone through as I sensed their suppressed sadness. Some of them were nonetheless filled with hopes about the future of Russia—even though they were the very people who had suffered at times untold moral or physical ordeals.

I made a special effort to meet as many older artists and writers as I could. As far as painting was concerned, I was anxious to have a glimpse of what the spirit of Russian art had been between 1910 and 1925. Artists of approximately Boris Pasternak's generation had been able then to absorb Western art traditions by studying in France or in Germany. Their training, together with the revolutionary ferment of the first decades of this century, created in Russia a daring modern art. In 1927, all independent groupings of artists were forbidden and modern art ended in the USSR.

Nowadays, one can see samples of it only in museum store-rooms (fairly easily accessible to the public at the time of my visit in Moscow, although not officially open) and in private collections. The words of Malevich, of Kandin-sky, early Chagall, and those of lone wolfs like the surrealist Paul Filonov are avidly sought after by many Russian col-lectors. Incidentally, Russian art collecting operates on a closed circuit. Importing, and especially exporting, of art is severely regulated, but within the established limitations, trading is active, encompassing every kind of art available in the USSR (chiefly works from private collections which were thrown on the market during the Revolution). Icons are especially fashionable right now.

One of my most pleasant afternoons in Moscow was spent in the studio of the late painter Robert Falk. Falk died in 1958, but many of his works are still assembled in his studio. Those comfortable well-lighted quarters overlook the site of a nineteenth-century church which Stalin had blown up in the early thirties—a spot now occupied by a heated swimming pool.

The works of Falk, lovingly shown to guests by his widow, are the negation of all dark forces in life. It is a mas-culine and yet gentle art: Falk was inspired by Cézanne and Modigliani and created a lyrical, sustained hymn to the intimacy and beauty of nature and people. Falk's canvases constitute one of the most perfect ensembles of paintings to be seen in Moscow. His views of the Russian countryside and of the environs of Moscow are so attentive to the sweetness of the landscape that one can't help being moved. I left Falk's studio with an enhanced love for Russia and respect for a painter who retained enough strength and inspiration to go on with his work through a long era of deprivation and turmoil. There must have been periods during the war when canvases and paints could not be procured, except perhaps through miracles of devotion on the part of the artist's wife and friends.

"Poetry, the art of the heart, withstood adversity best," Evtushenko had said, and on the whole this seemed to be true. What I knew of the revolutionary painting and sculpture, the modern works of the twenties, was so unconnected with present-day Moscow that it was like a relic out of a very ancient past. Primarily this is the result of a deeply felt Russian emphasis on content in art, not just on the part of narrow-minded officials, but of accomplished artists.

As a result of this attitude, the most interesting young Soviet artists are not inspired by the Russian art of the twenties, neither are they really influenced by reproductions of abstract-expressionist works. Instead, they try to recapture the experiences of the recent Russian past in terms of a new kind of expressionism. Their art is often crude, but it is sometimes effective because of the dramatic subject matter and the sincerity of the artists. Thus in the relatively free atmosphere of the 1960's a new kind of art seems to be in the making in the USSR—a "new realism" which is both more emotional and more plastic than the traditional Soviet Socialist realism. Neizvestni's sculptures point to this trend. And today a whole group of young painters under the direction of Elie Beliutin appear to be working in this new direction. Elie Beliutin, a painter in his late thirties, teaches at Moscow's Institute of Graphic Arts; his classes are often held out of doors. He is an inspired teacher and his students are devoted to him. Under his direction they are able to establish a direct contact with the natural world, bypassing both the clichés of socialist realism and those of Western abstraction. Their works, not derivative of anything in particular, are impressive. They unite the two-dimensionality of Russian icons with a genuine concern for subject matter, be it the human figure or a landscape. The "Beliutinzi," as Beliutin's students are called in Moscow, work in brilliant colors, use large simplified shapes, abstract their subjects, yet their pictures remain realistic. They are moving: it is as if the recent sufferings of the Russian people had suddenly begun to find an expression in painting. The "Beliutinzi" are at present tolerated by the Soviet government. They occasionally hold small public showings in Moscow, always as a group, for they are animated by a strong *esprit de corps*. They might well constitute the embryo of a new Soviet school of art.

Of course, the works of certain older Soviet artists do exert their influence on the young generation, for example the paintings of Robert Falk and the sculptures of Dmitri Tzaplin, who keeps his statues of dark animals, fishes, birds, lions in a somber studio lost in an ancient-looking back alley in the center of Moscow. The water-colorist Von Vizin is another artist with a following: young people often come to his small apartment where he willingly displays some examples of his immense output of water colors. His people and flowers and landscapes remind one of Dufy, yet they are intensely personal with their shimmering colors and their childlike, ever renewed freshness.

The engraver Vladimir Favorsky is another elderly but vital Moscow artist. He is now nearing eighty and has a big white beard like Tolstoi's and eyes of amazing luminosity. Favorsky is the master of Russian black and white illustration. He has worked as a wood engraver without interruption since the early years of the century, illustrating books with a talent unequaled in the USSR, where book illustration is a lively art. Surrounded by a large family of children and grandchildren he lives in a country house outside of Moscow. When he built this house many years ago, it was lost in the countryside; now it is part of a growing suburb. I called on him one evening, having walked several kilometers out of town past the last subway stop. I didn't know just how far beyond the outskirts of Moscow the artist lived. I walked for a long time in the snow, through barely lit tree-lined streets, in a secluded area of small houses and gardens. When I finally reached his house, Favorsky gave me some boiling tea to warm me up and showed me his marvelous illustrations for Pushkin's *Small Dramas in Verse*, which he was just finishing. Those small engravings contained more historical sense, greater scope than all the large historical paintings at the Tretyakovka put together. Yet they were completely modern. Favorsky illustrated and designed many books in the Akademia series, published during the twenties and early thirties. Now in his small house, bent over his boards, Favorsky fills one with a feeling of the continuity of Russia. This patriarch working on his engravings seems to have stepped out of a time when Russia was still a wooded immensity and all its houses were wooden and men wore big beards.

We in the West regard the nineteenth century as a distant epoch, we stylize it in our minds. But for the main stream of Russian culture, unaffected by Freud, by Kafka, by Stravinsky, the nineteenth century was yesterday. The majority of Russians do not experience the modern hell of daily confrontation with meticulous accounts of every disaster and crisis. Their world view is still relatively one-sided. It is a difficult situation under which to create an art with a universal appeal. For this reason, artists like Ernst Neizvestni who are able to express a theme of general concern make a great contribution to their country's intellectual life. So do the older writers who help maintain a tradition of nineteenth-century Russian universality, as Konstantin Paustovsky does, for example. I didn't meet him while in Moscow—he was vacationing in the Crimea—but we corresponded. Here are a few lines from one of his letters:

Yalta, January 1960

"I am writing these lines in Yalta, precisely when the centenary of one of the most humane people ever to live on earth is about to be celebrated. Chekhov spent a long time in Yalta. From my window I see his house on a slope. Here in Yalta I often think about Chekhov and the hard road before an artist . . .

"I am full of hope that the writers of the United States, when they come to know us Russian writers, will become the friends of many of us, sharing those thoughts that inspire or delight us or fill us with indignation.

"I like contemporary Americans and their fathers and grandfathers, the marvelous pioneers of America . . . From my early childhood I envied Tom Sawyer and Huckleberry Finn. Those provincial boys have become eternal figures equal in scope to Don Quixote and Sancho Panza."

EHRENBURG:

Portrait of a Writer
as Intellectual

10 / Ehrenburg on Painting

Thy sky rolled snowdrifts,
Masses of troubled night.
You and the mountainous sky
Were of an essence.

Through the deserted side streets
And the stalactites of caverns
The R of your name—how proudly!—
Rolls and repeats and resounds.

Caught between sky and palate,
Ehrenburg, doubter, rejoice!
In the dream-spun snowdrifts
Your name rolls and resounds. . . .

> —MARINA TSVETAYEVA from "Snowdrifts,"
> a poem dedicated to Ilya Ehrenburg in 1921

While in Moscow, I met a writer who is almost
as well known there as Sholokhov, but for very different
reasons. Sholokhov portrays the Russian earth while Ilya
Ehrenburg stands for worldly refinement; in the eyes of the
Russian reader he is an intellectual par excellence.

I telephoned Ehrenburg a few days after my arrival in

Moscow. I had heard him speak the year before at a public meeting in Geneva. Though he seemed dead tired, his eyes half shut with fatigue, his voice raspy at times, his performance had been moving. In French tinged with a noticeable Russian accent, he spoke about the impending horror of atomic warfare.

"Ilya Grigorievich has to be 'avaricious' with his time," said his secretary in answer to my morning call. "He is so occupied . . . But I shall convey your message to him." Later that day, just after I had returned to the Metropole from a chilled but dazzling first walk along the windy quays of the frozen Moskva River, she called back to say that Ehrenburg had agreed to see me briefly. A date was set for the following week.

Ehrenburg's home and office are at Number 8 Gorki Street, four or five blocks from Red Square, in the center of town. Gorki Street is Moscow's major thoroughfare. It is a commercial street, wide and straight. Many of its stores stay open in the evening. It is lined with movie theaters and cafés; knowing teenagers refer to it as Broadway. Ehrenburg's apartment is high up in a large apartment house that has a bookstore on the street floor. On one side the store opens onto a square where pigeons, undisturbed by the cold weather, perch irreverently on a bronze statue of Yuri Dolgoruki, the mythical founder of Moscow. In the tiny square, Yuri, his helmeted head bent, rides an oversized black horse. Across the square there is a coffee shop with a pink neon sign over the entrance. This is a good place to meet someone for lunch, since the service there is a great improvement over that usually found at restaurants in the big Moscow hotels.

When I went to see Ehrenburg for the first time, there was a crowd of people both inside and around the bookstore, although it was quite late in the day. A book on impressionism had gone on sale that week. It was displayed in the window: a thick volume with a reproduction on the cover of a Renoir lady holding a fan. Bookstores are numerous in Moscow but are nonetheless always filled with customers. Mobs of avid shoppers crowd about simple counters piled high with volumes of every size and shape. I had also seen classics sold from makeshift tables on the snowy sidewalks—modestly dressed Muscovites were lined up in the sub-zero weather waiting for their turn to purchase newly printed volumes still smelling of ink.

The bookstore on Gorki Street was more elaborate than most. Large and well-lighted, it displayed books against a background of brightly colored pegboard. The various counters were clearly marked—Education, Sciences, Art—and the store was provided with an adequate number of salespeople. A vast assortment of art postcards filled an entire corner of the store. Most of them were genre paintings from Russian museums and there were many Victorian favorites familiar to me despite my foreign education: Ivan Shishkin's *Family of Bears* and Constantin Flavitsky's *Princess Tarakanova* perishing in her prison. (She was an unfortunate rival of Empress Catherine the Great. The legend is that she was drowned in the Peter and Paul Fortress in a spring flood of the Neva. She is shown in her dungeon cell, cringing in terror on her bed as the waters rise around her.) I also saw several reproductions of impressionist works. Now that they are no longer censored by the authorities, they are becoming increasingly popular in the Soviet Union.

I leafed through the book on impressionism. For a Soviet art publication it was well executed and the color reproductions were better than usual. I also noticed a display of a paperbound book about Andrei Rublev. It was a handsome book but still inexpensive, like all Soviet publications. It contained a text by one of the leading Russian art critics, Professor M. V. Alpatov. It looked like a good present to take to friends in the West. Its cover, a detail from an icon showing a dark golden angel with pensive brown eyes, had caught my attention before in windows of other bookstores, but I hesitated to buy it since an earlier attempt at shopping in Moscow had proved too complicated. This was soon after my arrival in Moscow when I ran out of aspirin. I had a slight cold and set out in search of a pharmacy. I discovered a vast, state-operated establishment situated in a dilapidated town house behind the Metropole. Its two floors, linked by a sweeping staircase, were jammed with customers. They seemed to be rushing in different directions as if in some sort of panic.

I soon learned that buying aspirin would require several intricate steps. The shopping system, possibly an inheritance from the times when goods were scarcer in the USSR, is as follows: first, one lines up in front of counters bearing goods to find out the price of what one wants. Then there is a trip to the cashiers to buy a ticket, which in turn will allow one to receive the merchandise after going through a third waiting line. Rather than undertake the struggle, it was simpler to go back to the hotel and get into bed.

The bookstore on Gorki Street, however, was run more smoothly, and after only a little waiting I had my four copies of Rublev. As I left the store, I suddenly realized that it was later than I thought. I had to find Ehrenburg's place immediately. It was already the hour set for the appointment.

Number 8 Gorki Street is composed of several apartment buildings arranged around a courtyard; they occupy a whole city block. The courtyard, white and deserted, had only a few small paths dug through the snow, leading to several unmarked doors. A low wall topped by rusted grillework enclosed one side of the courtyard. Past the grille I could see a typical Moscow landscape. One is often struck by such views, which usually appear at the end of an old alley or between high fences. There were snowy roofs, tall reddish brick walls and an old log house. All this in ir-regular clusters broken by white spaces, houses set at strange angles, a feeling of informality, almost of abandon.

There was no listing of tenants or apartments to be seen anywhere. Because of previous experiences, I was re-luctant to approach the concierge, one of those downcast women wrapped in shawls the color of dust who seem peculiar to Moscow. They usually doze, sitting in the dark-ness near the elevator. These old women seem to delib-erately put out of their minds the names of the tenants. They are, or pretend to be, deaf to one's questions. They refuse either to be wakened from their slumber or inter-rupted in their knitting. Perhaps their withdrawal is a vestige of darker days when people wanted to preserve their anonymity as much as possible. Or was it my slight foreign accent that put them on their guard? Locating someone's apartment is often hard in Moscow even if one has a cor-rect number. Because there is never adequate marking, the search may turn into a Kafkaesque dream—dark stairways, cold, unkempt landings, wrong doors, broken bells and crawling, ancient elevators which can be operated only by a special key in the possession of the concierge.

As I looked for the right entrance the brick wall in the courtyard was turning redder from the setting sun and the snow reflected a brilliant pink. I was growing more dis-tressed at the thought of being late to Ehrenburg's.

Ehrenburg has the reputation of being one of the busiest of all the Muscovite writers.

Making a desperate guess, I selected at random one stairway entrance. To my great relief it turned out to be the right one, and soon a maid was letting me into Ehrenburg's warm apartment. An irascible small dog inspected me and retired after barking once or twice.

It was like entering another world: I found myself in a place totally unlike the typical Moscow dwelling. It was airy. It looked like the home of a well-to-do artistic Parisian intellectual. The furniture was comfortable and inconspicuous. The drawings and paintings in Ehrenburg's collection were mostly French and many of them bore friendly inscriptions to Ehrenburg from the artists. There were many black and whites by Picasso which gave the place an overall luminosity. Here and there a Chagall or a Léger added a note of vibrant color which matched the tones of brightly patterned scatter rugs. The cushions on the sofa were covered with handwoven folk materials—purple, deep blue, yellow. Pictures filled the living room and continued on into a hall. Through a half-closed door I could see even more of them in an adjoining room.

Mme. Ehrenburg, Lubov Mikhailovna, is a statuesque dark-haired woman. She is still quite beautiful and dresses with an understated elegance which is rare in Moscow. She is affable but reserved, and slow in her movements. Years before, she had met my father in Berlin and remembered him as a handsome poet with black hair. Lubov Mikhailovna, a painter, once studied with the Russian constructivist Rodchenko. Two small canvases of her own which she later showed at my insistence were painted in an expressionist manner and had an individual grace.

Noting my interest in painting, she led me on a brief

tour of the collection. She took a few additional works out of a closet, including several Léger lithographs from the series *Les Constructeurs*. Compared to Moscow's wintry existence with its soft diffused light and its lack of visual richness in clothes and furnishings, these works sparkled. There were French workers in bright blue overalls carrying yellow and red rafters; Picasso's fauns and nude girls dancing—one could almost hear their tambourines and hoof-beats. Ehrenburg had several drawings and lithographs of the master's unsurpassed series of the early nineteen-fifties. A thoughtful gypsy, a Spaniard draped in a dark cloak, a playful monkey, looked down from the wall. I had a sudden yearning for the light-heartedness of the Latins. In my few days in Moscow I had already become aware of the moody intensity of the Russian people, deeply concerned with the future of their country and of the world, filled at once with high hopes and high indignation. By contrast the Picasso dancers, the Infanta in a big white collar, and a young mother looked self-contained, completely at peace with the world.

There were also, of course, Russian works in Ehrenburg's collection. I noticed an early Chagall self-portrait, severe and incisive, painted in Russia during the artist's early and most forceful period. In the small bedroom Lubov Mikhailovna showed me a later Chagall, a small nude, more luxuriant in color. Its pinks were complemented by a beautiful icon hanging beside it.

Mme. Ehrenburg took obvious pleasure in showing me some Picasso jewelry made of clay and her collection of scarves designed by Léger, Matisse, and Picasso in commemoration of various political rallies.

She told me the story of a fragment of sculpture standing in the living room. It had been found shortly after the

Revolution by a student, a friend and protégé of Ilya Grigorievich's, in the vicinity of the Zubov estate, a famous Russian eighteenth-century palace. A crowd of little boys were kicking the stone around, and he rescued it. Later, Ehrenburg inherited the sculpture. It has a Greek inscription on its side but Ehrenburg has never found time to have it authenticated. The sculpture blends perfectly with his collection, Mediterranean in feeling.

We talked about collecting—what a strong impulse it is, especially among Russians in spite of the crowded conditions in which so many of them live. Mme. Ehrenburg told me of several art collections she had seen recently, of both old and modern works, assembled by people in modest circumstances. She mentioned some of the problems of preserving and displaying Ilya Grigorievich's pictures. Gorki Street is one of the most heavily traveled streets in Moscow. It is one of the city's main bus routes. Parades frequently march up Gorki Street on the way to Red Square; trucks shake the walls of the buildings. Elegant as the apartment itself is, the walls are thin, the plaster sometimes falls off in big pieces. Paintings tumble down, their glass and frames shattered. Lubov Mikhailovna had recently devised a system for supporting them safely: a thin tubing, painted the same white as the walls, is attached to the ceiling and runs along the four walls. The pictures are hung from it. They are arranged with taste, sometimes in clusters of two or three works of similar technique one above the other. Old Russian and Ukrainian ceramic folk toys on a shelf resemble the Picasso fauns: brightly striped rams with oversized curved horns, small horses, imaginary beasts, all hoofs and horns.

After a while Ehrenburg's secretary came in. Ilya Grigorievich was ready to see me, but not for long, as he was expecting someone else in a short while. She mentioned the name of Boris Slutzky, a well-known Soviet poet.

Ilya Ehrenburg is rather tall, slightly bent by age, with a mop of hair which was well known in his Montparnasse days (he once had a postcard safely delivered to him at the Rotonde addressed only: "For the man with the uncombed hair.") His hair is now dark gray with white streaks. His eyes are exceedingly sharp yet somehow uncurious. As I stepped into his study I saw a drawing of him on the far wall. It was a pencil portrait, inscribed: "*Pour toi mon ami, Picasso, 29 août 1948.*" Brief as this sketch was, it captured Ehrenburg's cold intelligence. A few pencil strokes and everything about Ehrenburg was there: a slightly brooding expression—what the French call *le regard lourd*—with something also of a bird of prey. Picasso had caught him in a moment of concentration. But there is nothing introverted in that concentration; rather, Ehrenburg looks like a haughty old warrior, as one would imagine the chieftain of a Caucasian mountain tribe described by Lermontov.

It is a strange feeling to have a person's very essence displayed thus on the wall, and I found myself unconsciously checking with it as the acquaintance progressed. I began to feel that there were three people in the room: Ehrenburg, myself, and this other Ehrenburg, Picasso's, a younger man, more of a cynic.

Yet there is something attractive in Ehrenburg's hauteur; he does not smile, there is no display of friendliness or interest on his part, no hostility either. I sensed that he found me an inexperienced conversationalist, but he was patient. I became more and more absorbed in observing my host.

I was beginning to comprehend the significance of a man who until then was mostly a name to me, a name I had often heard mentioned since childhood. I had read his novels without quite being able to form an image of their author. Suddenly I thought I knew how Ehrenburg, without a profusion of artistic gifts but with exceptional intelligence and critical sense, came to be an important writer. He has that self-confidence, that arrogance perhaps, which makes a man presumptuous enough to believe that he has something to say to the world, not through an occasional flash of creativity but through persistent effort, long enough to build a life's work. Ehrenburg is not a great writer, probably because his imagination is limited, but he is a serious writer. He has understood and lived the ideas and the events of his epoch and has persevered in recording them. Such a writer contributes to the shaping of literature. His works open new possibilities for other artists: through his novels Ehrenburg is able to indicate just what is important at the moment.

The conversation turned to the interview which Ehrenburg had given Norman Cousins shortly before my visit to Moscow. It revolved around the relationship of writers with their readers, both in the United States and in the USSR. Ehrenburg's interest in his readers is well known. Alfred Kazin has said, for instance, that Ehrenburg emphasized the extent of his following among the Soviet people to boost his own ego: "It is hard listening to Ehrenburg talk about how many letters he gets each week to suppress thoughts of movie stars, and TV comedians . . ." Perhaps only other Russians can appreciate just how sincere and well-advised the pedagogical impulse is among the majority of Russian writers. Throughout the nineteenth and early twentieth centuries, writers able to foresee the outcome of the Czarist policies of oppression and enforced ignorance, concerned themselves intently with the welfare and education of the masses. But in the immense and decadent Empire there were too few such people to prevent the ultimate disasters. In an effort to awaken the upper classes to the misery of the Russian people, Tolstoi and Gorki were deeply absorbed in public life, in "community action" as it is called in Russian. Nineteenth-century tradition considers "community action" a moral imperative for writers. Ehrenburg is directly in line with this tradition. Thus, far from being frivolous, his mention of the number of letters he receives from readers refers to a conscious attempt on his part to create public awareness in Russia outside of the established political and academic channels. He is trying to encourage the public to form opinions and to make these opinions heard—in letters, in newspapers, at meetings. This attempt should not be misunderstood, and much depends on its success.

The lamps were turned on in Ehrenburg's study. It was a small and comfortable room, located on the courtyard side of the apartment, the quieter side. There were books everywhere, and a wide blue couch was placed against one wall. Ehrenburg sat in a deep armchair near his desk. I settled on the edge of the couch. I was looking at Ehrenburg, his slightly stooped, massive figure, his profile outlined against the window, through which the late day was still visible. Ehrenburg mentioned Tsvetayeva, who had been a great friend of his. A passionate admirer of Tsvetayeva's poetry, he has been instrumental in procuring her recognition in the Soviet Union. He said that he expected a selection of her poems to be published in 1961.* Then we talked about painting; I was under the spell of the art works I had just

---

* This much-awaited book was published in Moscow in the fall of 1961. An excellent selection, it demonstrated Tsvetayeva's scope as a lyric poet. Indeed, she is one of Russia's greatest poets, endowed with a singular ability to feel and describe an immense variety of human experiences. She had naturally the universality for which Pasternak strived. The publication of her verse was one of the major literary events of 1961 in the USSR.

seen. I had been in Moscow long enough to realize that it was often impossible to communicate with Russians on matters of art appreciation; people whose taste in books or music were very much akin to my own spoke a different language when it came to painting. Ehrenburg, however, having witnessed in Paris all the most important developments in the art of our century, has a special understanding of modern art which can be formed only in painters' studios and through intimate association with the painters themselves. At one time in his youth he had painted himself. I looked around Ehrenburg's study. It was a room even more French than the other rooms, with rare leather-bound editions and white French paperbacks among hard-bound Russian volumes. Ehrenburg owns an edition of Ronsard published in 1579. There were two paintings of Paris hanging near the desk: a small Marquet representing the quays of the Seine, and a Parisian street by Robert Falk, painted in soft, grayish colors.

Ehrenburg told me that almost all the works he owned were gifts from the artists and that there were more in his country house. I mentioned my lack of knowledge about Russian contemporary art. He recommended I see a show of portraits then being held by the Painters' Union. It was a closed show; only members of the Painters' Union and a few invited guests were admitted. It had been assembled "for purposes of study for the members of the Union." I went to this exhibit, using Ehrenburg's name, and found it one of the liveliest shows of modern Soviet art in Moscow. It included many works by painters who were ostracized in the thirties and forties as well as works by young artists of promise.

Ehrenburg took me around the apartment to give me a chance to examine once more the Russian works he owned.

He pointed out a romantic portrait of a girl in a big hat by Alexander Tishler, somehow reminiscent of Eugene Berman. Like Berman, Tishler is well known for his stage sets. Tishler came originally from Kiev, where there was an active school of painting in the early twenties. Subsequently, several of its members worked for the theater. I saw a lovely head by the sculptress Sarah Lebedeva, whom Ehrenburg suggested I go and see in her studio. To my regret, her illness made this visit impossible. Ehrenburg unrolled a red cubistic composition by David Shterenberg, a friend of his during the Montparnasse years. It was a characteristic cubist still life, of a fish and a wire *panier à salade*. I then stopped near the Parisian scene by Robert Falk, another Paris-trained Russian painter. Ehrenburg said that Falk's soft, luminous paintings of nature, his lyric still lifes, look their best in the country, in a setting of greenery and flowers in bloom.

He also spoke about the painter Martiros Sarian, an Armenian whom he particularly liked, and about a whole group of artists working in Armenia, mostly colorists inspired by the landscape and the southern light. Sarian had recently completed a portrait of Ehrenburg, of which I saw a black and white photograph. Judging by this reproduction, it is rather heavily painted and fails to do justice to the finesse of Ehrenburg's features—though perhaps the omnipresent Picasso sketch made me judge Sarian's portrait too severely.

I asked Ehrenburg whether he could tell me anything about the young painters in Moscow. Who in his opinion had outstanding talent? He led me back to his study and sat down again in the armchair. "Unfortunately, young Russian artists are in a difficult position today," he said in his articulate, patient manner. "Painting, like all other arts, relies on a continuity of experience. More than anything, young painters and sculptors need to know the works of their immediate elders. There has not been a sufficient degree of continuity because the once flourishing Russian school of painting suffered from the political events of the time. Thus our younger artists lack the benefit of a tradition, a thing essential to the growth of an artist. It is imperative that our better artists be exhibited more widely for the sake of their younger colleagues.

"I am happy to say," he went on, "that there were recent showings of Robert Falk, of David Shterenberg, of the water colorist Von Vizin. Also, everything should be done to present more good foreign art to Soviet audiences. I feel that one important contribution in this direction was made by the large Picasso show held in Moscow in 1956, which was an immense success. But as far as the painters of your generation are concerned, too often I find their works only tentative."

There was a muted shuffling and then a noise of barking in the hall. Evidently my host's next visitor had arrived. Before getting up to leave, I gave Ehrenburg a paperbound edition of the *Writers at Work* collection, and suggested he might like to leaf through it.

I rose and thanked Ilya Grigorievich and said I hoped I might see him again and talk to him about his writing. It was a fairly unrealistic hope: Ehrenburg on the whole had been rather distant.

I stepped into the cold blue evening. The bookstore was still full of animation, but the pigeons had deserted Yuri Dolgoruki, now a dark mass against the sky. Reflections from the neon signs on Gorki Street dotted the snow with pink and green light. I walked to the café across the square and ordered a supper of tea, caviar, and oranges: these foods were especially satisfying in the cold weather. In my notebook I wrote down as many names as I could remember of those mentioned by Ilya Grigorievich, for I resolved to go the next day to the Tretyakov Gallery, Moscow's museum of Russian art. I also wanted to meet a few of Moscow's artists. I had known Russian painters in Paris, but then, their art had become quite Parisian. I wondered how painting had evolved in an isolated environment, so completely unlike the West, where an "international art school" has developed as a result of the free circulation of artistic ideas.

11 / Ehrenburg on Writing

Come celebrate, kinsmen, the twilight of freedom,
The darkening conscience, the great year obscured;
Into the boiling waters of nightfall
A heavy forest of nets is let down.
The days of your rising are numb,
O sun, judge, people!

Into battle legions we have tied the swallows.
Day is invisible, the whole element
Sings, whirrs, lives . . .
Between the nets clouded with twilight
The sun is dark and the land goes sailing.

Those who have heart must know, O Time,
Your boat is sinking to the bottom.

Still, let us try a turn of the wheel—
Clumsy, rasping, enormous—
Dividing the ocean like a driven plough
We will remember when Lethe is frozen
That life to us was worth ten heavens.

> —OSIP MANDELSTAM, "The Twilight of Free-
> dom," 1918, from *Tristia*

A few days after my visit to Gorki Street, Ehrenburg's secretary called me to say that after looking at the *Writers at Work* collection Ilya Grigorievich had agreed to answer a few questions. This interview was postponed several times—Ehrenburg was especially busy because of the Supreme Soviet. As days and weeks elapsed I began to fear that it would not take place at all. In the meantime, however, I tried to find out just what my Muscovite acquaintances thought about Ehrenburg. I soon realized that he was universally respected among the painters and the poets for his opinions. As a writer he seemed better liked for his essays than his novels, although those who had read *Julio Jurenito*—not reprinted in the USSR in recent years—greatly admired it. His role as a cultural intermediary with France was well known and was considered desirable, reflecting as it does the profound Russian empathy for France. But Ehrenburg's audience is not at all limited to an élite. I was told that shortly before my visit to Moscow a tremendous controversy had stirred Soviet public opinion—in fact, it was still going on. In October, 1959, Ehrenburg published an article in *Komsomolskaya Pravda*, which is a daily newspaper devoted primarily to the Komsomols, the Soviet youth who undertake the first step towards becoming Party members by joining the Komsomol Youth Organization. In recent years this group has lost some of its political significance since the number of Komsomols has vastly increased, and today the 3,400,000 readers of *Komsomolskaya Pravda* are recruited from every age group of Soviet society. One of the most popular features of this newspaper is the lively column of letters received from readers.

Ehrenburg's article dealt with the relationship between the arts and sciences and quoted a letter which he had recently received, signed "Nina." An anonymous young woman had just broken up with Yuri, her fiancé, because he criticized and mocked her interest in the arts. He was himself a scientist, tolerant only of sciences. Through the newspaper, Nina was asking Ilya Grigorievich's opinion: Was her passion for art an error? Is art as important as science? Does it have a place in modern society? Ehrenburg's answer was of course that Yuri was misled, that art was as alive and as needed as ever. It was a good instance of Ehrenburg's pedagogical role. His article started a far-reaching controversy: *Komsomolskaya Pravda* received thousands of letters, about ten thousand in all. Nina became something of a symbol, and the overwhelming majority of the readers felt that Yuri had wronged her, that he was narrow-minded and misinformed. There were public meetings organized to discuss the problem. At one of them, held in a workers' club on the Avenue of the Enthusiasts in Moscow—a thoroughfare leading east to Siberia and named for the revolutionaries who in Czarist times started their journey to exile along it—Ehrenburg successfully confounded a well-known professor of the Moscow Institute of Cybernetics who spoke in favor of Yuri's point of view. There were more letters, and in January Ehrenburg wrote another article which closed the debate triumphantly for the humanistic point of view. The scope of the debate, its naïveté, its earnestness were so Russian! I thought it might be interesting to ask Ehrenburg about it. When Ehrenburg's secretary called me to say that Ilya Grigorievich could see me the next day, I prepared a few questions centered around this theme. I was tempted to approach the interview spontaneously, without questions prepared in advance, but remembering Ehrenburg's reserved manner I decided against it. It might have been a mistake; if I had been less formal myself, the ice might have been broken. It wasn't.

The interview took place on the morning before Ehrenburg's departure for Stockholm and lasted a little more than an hour. We sat in the living room among all the Picassos.

Ilya Grigorievich was preoccupied but he gave precise, rapidly spoken answers to my questions. I took notes as he went along. His secretary, a lovely, cultivated woman, subsequently helped me transcribe my notes: Ilya Grigorievich wanted his words recorded with complete exactness. The interview was interrupted by phone calls—one of them was from Ehrenburg's doctor. It was at the height of the Moscow smallpox scare: Ilya Grigorievich, who had not yet taken the time to be vaccinated, could not leave the USSR without being immunized, but every minute before his departure was accounted for and it seemed almost impossible to fit a doctor's appointment into his tight schedule. I began to feel that the hour he devoted to me was a generous gesture on his part.

As we sat down, I asked Ilya Grigorievich about his article in *Komsomolskaya Pravda*. What were his reasons for starting the controversy about Nina's letter?

"The problem I was concerned with is that of excessive specialization," he said in his slightly weary, patient tone. "I have seen it among American technicians. My article was written to warn our youth about the dangers of one-sided growth. The role of the arts in society I would link closely with the problem of educating the sentiments—of *L'Education Sentimentale*, as Flaubert called it. I must tell you that even before my article was published there was a movement among our youth to try to round out their education in this respect. A couple of years ago I attended the inauguration of the first 'University of Culture' at one of the advanced technical institutions in Moscow. Young people studying electrical engineering assembled to form a club, the 'University of Culture,' to find out more about painting, music, and the other arts. Such clubs are now being formed in every university."

I asked Ilya Grigorievich how he reconciled the activities of a writer with those of a political figure—a question which particularly interested me, since I knew that political engagement is an absolute imperative for a Soviet writer.

"This is closely related to your first question. I feel that in our time a poet should have an understanding of nuclear physics and a physicist should enjoy poetry. Of course science has become so advanced that a Goethe or a Leonardo, specialists in both the arts and sciences, are unfortunately inconceivable. But I cannot imagine a writer these days who would write a novel shut up in his study. I know they do exist. I think that they show how fruitless literary craft is unless the author actively experiences what happens to his hero. There is Flaubert's view, held in his youth: 'If you want to describe courage, do not become a soldier; a lover, do not fall in love; a drunkard, do not drink wine.' There is also a brilliant refutation of this theory, Stendhal. He was a soldier, drank and made love, and was marvelously successful at describing a variety of human passions. I do not draw a line between my literary work and my political activity because I defend the same ideas in both. I cannot understand why the defense of man against atomic death should be left to professional diplomats. It's as much a writer's concern, since a writer is responsible to his readers for all the books written before him as well as those which will be written after him. I also do not understand why some feel that cultural exchanges should be put in the hands of political leaders who already have too much to attend to.

"To tell the truth, I find your question strange. I would like to ask you—or rather ask American writers: do they find it possible to 'just be writers' at a time when it is necessary to both create and defend literature?"

"But isn't it difficult practically to conciliate writing with public service?"

"We are coming back to your first question. Some people assert that a present-day engineer cannot read novels or listen to music—he does not have time for these things. I want to remind you of a man whom I knew—you knew him too, I understand, who has left his mark on modern science. I am thinking of Frédéric Joliot-Curie. He was able to write his last work about radioactivity from the notes of Pierre Curie, to direct the construction of a scientific research center, to be the president of the International Peace Council, to paint, to enjoy music—all in the same years. Evidently our notion of time, of hours and days, is relative. Time narrows or expands according to how we approach it. It varies with a man's breadth, with his heart. There is that American saying—time is money. Time can be many other things—it can be the immortality of the individual. His short mortal life may broaden not only in time but in space as it expands into the life of society itself."

"What do you think of the novel as a literary form—of its future?"

"It seems to me that the novel is very much alive as a form. Without any question, every epoch has its own forms, and the novel nowadays cannot resemble that of the nineteenth century. In this domain all experiments are justified, and it is better to write something new clumsily than to repeat the old brilliantly. In the nineteenth century, novels dealt with the fate of a person or of a family; this was linked to life in that period. In our time the destinies of people are interwoven. Whether man recognizes it or not, his fate is much more linked to that of many other people than it used to be. This modifies the architecture of the novel where, as in the film, there is a succession of close-ups and crowd shots. I have tried to approach novels in various ways, leaving the old notion of building up a character, on which traditional novels are based. I have written a satirical novel which is part essay and part history, *Julio Jurenito*. Some of my other novels are conceived as chronicles of our times—but humanized chronicles, unlike those of historians or sociologists. Such is my novel, *The Second Day*.

"In others, I have tried to approach my subject matter as a poet would. In such cases the most important thing for me was not the fate of individual heroes, but rather a certain situation, a mood. Such are *Summer of 1925* and *The Thaw*. But even in those novels which are more like classical novels —like *The Fall of Paris* and *The Tempest*—my attention was not concentrated on given heroes, but on those central elements which are the real heroes of those novels—Paris in the case of *The Fall of Paris*, the war in *The Tempest*. I have already told you that in my opinion the most important thing for the writer is an ability to live the experiences of his heroes—to "co-experience" them. We must abandon the notion that a writer is only an observer—he is not a camera. He is expected to present that which is invisible at first. He must reveal the inner world of man, and that is possible only if the writer has experienced something similar to what he describes. This is the only way for him to really understand his heroes."

"Who are your favorite authors among classic writers, among Soviet writers, and among the foreign ones?"

"Among the classics, Chekhov and Stendhal are the closest to me. Hemingway is the contemporary foreign writer I like best. Among the young Soviet writers, that is in prose, the most interesting are Victor Nekrassov, Vera Panova, Emmanuel Kazakevich, Vladimir Tendriakov, and the youngest of them, Yuri Kazakov."

"Who do you think deserves most to be translated?"

"I can't give you any advice there. It is like telling a shopper in a department store which fabric to buy. It is a

matter of taste, the shopper should follow his own inclina-
tions."

As Ehrenburg went on dictating the answers to my questions, speaking slowly and distinctly, he became more elliptic, glancing now and then at his watch. It was obvious he
felt the pressure of time and that the informal interview was
an impossibility. Four or five questions were what he expected and had answered, as detached as a teacher giving a
dictation class. I closed my notebook and said good-bye.
We shook hands. On my way out I met Mme. Ehrenburg in
the hall. She was getting her husband ready for his trip,
but she took a minute for a last chat. The hall was full of
potted, early spring flowers brought from the Ehrenburgs'
country house. In frozen Moscow those pale hyacinths and
tulip buds were my first glimpse of spring.

12 / Ehrenburg's Memoirs

There are no monuments on Babii Yar,
A steep ravine is all, a rough memorial.
Fear is my ground—
Old as the Jewish people, a Jew myself it seems,
I roam in Egypt in her ancient days,
I perish on the cross, and even now
I bear the red marks of nails.
I am Dreyfus, detested, denounced,
Snared behind prison bars:
Pettiness
Is my betrayer and my judge.
Shrieking ladies in fine ruffled gowns
Brandish their umbrellas in my face.

And now a boy in Bielostok,
I seem to see blood spurt and spread over the floor.
The tavern masters celebrate:
Under the smell of vodka and of onions
And of blood
Kicked by their heavy boots I lie
Begging in vain for pity.
The rampant pogrom roars
"Murder the Jews! Save Russia!"
A man is beating up my mother.

O Russian people,
I know your heart
Lives without bounds
But often men

With dirty hands abuse
The body of your clear name.
Shamelessly,
Without the quiver of a nerve
These pompous anti-Semites call themselves
"The union of the Russian people."

Anne Frank, I am she,
A translucent twig of April
And I am filled with love that needs no words.
We are forbidden the sky and the green leaves
But in this dark room we can embrace.
Ah, do not fear the noise—it is the rushing
Of spring itself
Come, let us kiss . . .
The sounds of thawing ice change to pounding on
*   the door.*

Wild grasses rustle over Babii Yar,
The trees stare down, stern as my judge,
Silent the air howls.
I bare my head, graying now,
And I am myself an endless soundless howl
Over the buried
Thousands and thousands of thousands,
And I am every old man shot down here
And every child.
In no limb of my body can I forget.

Let the Internationale
Be sung
When the last reviler of the Jews is dead.
No Jewish blood is mixed in mine, but let me be a
*   Jew*
For all anti-Semites to hate, to spit upon.
Only then I can call myself
Russian.

                    —EUGENE EVTUSHENKO, "Babii Yar," 1961

Outside Russia, Ehrenburg is sometimes criticized for somehow surviving Stalin's purges in the late forties. Yet there is no evidence that he caused anyone to suffer by remaining alive, and it is important to point out that Ehrenburg is respected by Jewish intellectuals in Russia. The fact that he is alive and active today appears to be a fortunate circumstance rather than a thing to begrudge him. Russians tend to think that the oppression which befell the entire country in the late forties was the result of one man's dark mania and not an organized discrimination against a specific group of people. The statistics that are available regarding earlier waves of oppressions show Stalin's determination to do away with all the intelligentsia, a group which included many Jews. He was successful to a great degree but not entirely: the tradition was strong enough to bring about the rebirth of an appreciable intellectual life after Stalin's death.

In Moscow I heard a story concerning Pasternak's survival. Whether this story in particular is true or not is relatively unimportant since it is similar to the many authentic ones which illustrate the atmosphere of blind whim prevailing at that time. It is said that Pasternak was spared because Stalin liked him personally and declared, as the poet was about to be arrested, "Let this cloud-dweller be."

Russian intellectuals, whether Jewish or not, remember Ehrenburg for his role in the early forties when he returned from German-invaded France. He was then the spokesman for anti-German feeling in the USSR, before the shift in Soviet policies. In France he had seen the atrocities of World War I at first hand, and from that time on he had a vitriolic hatred of Germany. He had a sense of historical perspective and was ardent in pointing out the extent of the Fascist threat. The prevailing opinion in Moscow is that Ehrenburg's political attitude today is diplomatic and dignified. Anti-Semitism is of great concern to Soviet intellectuals, as it is to Ehrenburg himself. Last year, in a speech to the Writers' Union on the occasion of his seventieth birthday, he said: "Whether this is agreeable or not to some, I am a Russian writer. But as long as there is one anti-Semite left, I will say and I will write in my passport: 'I am a Jew.'"

Ilya Ehrenburg is one of the most complex figures in contemporary Russian letters. He was shaped by the sweeping Russian events of this century. It is in the story of his life as it is told in his memoirs that he is more readily found.

He was born into a middle-class Jewish family, one which was quite assimilated. His father ran a brewery in Moscow. It was located next door to Tolstoi's town house. Today the two-story wooden house with its rustic fenced-in garden and the small red brick brewery are still standing on a side street of Moscow which exudes an old-fashioned urban torpor.

Ehrenburg recalls how Tolstoi once came over to the brewery to find out from his father how beer was made. Tolstoi had the utopian notion of getting the Russian people to switch from vodka to beer. Alcoholism, a serious ill in the Russia of those years, was of deep concern to the intelligentsia.

Ehrenburg grew up in Moscow and at sixteen he was already a revolutionary. Because of this he was expelled from the gymnasium and arrested a year later for underground activities. Miraculously, through a misunderstanding, he was allowed to leave for France in 1908. He went to Paris to study. There was then in Paris a so-called

First Russian Emigration. It was composed mostly of political exiles. Lenin was living near the Parc Montsouris and Ehrenburg met him shortly after his arrival. Paris had become a place of refuge for revolutionaries, anarchists, and liberals of many nationalities. Many foreign artists and writers were also living there. The atmosphere of this colony was mainly one of dedication to liberal ideas and art. This was to be true also of the post-revolutionary Emigration, that to which my parents belonged. Unfortunately, uncompromising monarchists were often the most outspoken group of the Second Emigration. They tended to give the whole colony the character of a petty small town: they were clannish and spent most of their time sighing for the good old days, the lost estates, their diamonds and servants, hoping that a miracle would restore the Romanoffs and their former privileges.

Paris proved to be a stimulating environment for Ehrenburg. He spent most of his time among the bohemians of those days—painters and writers later to be known as the "School of Paris," who were living around Montparnasse and Montmartre. The *douceur de vivre* of the turn of the century still pervaded Parisian life, but new art and new ideas—some of them very radical indeed—were being born. Ehrenburg became a friend of Picasso, Modigliani, Soutine, Diego Rivera. He met Guillaume Apollinaire, Max Jacob, Jean Cocteau, Blaise Cendrars. Everybody in this group of young men was extremely poor. A café-crème at the Rotonde, where writers often worked and artists congregated, sometimes had to last all day. Ehrenburg recalls that his room was so cold at night that he put layers of newspapers under his overcoat to try to keep warm.

In this atmosphere Ehrenburg began to write poetry. His Bolshevik sympathies never subsided, but he discovered a world wholly new to him, the world of art. He became absorbed in painting and in poetry. He published several books of poems in Russian and also made translations from French.

During World War I Ehrenburg worked as a war correspondent for a Russian newspaper. He observed the war first hand and, like many other writers of his generation—Sholokhov, Hemingway, Remarque—was filled with horror at what he saw. He was equally appalled by the hysterical and bigoted patriotism exploited by the French bourgeoisie in the first part of the war. Skepticism, a dominant trait of his character, was strong in him even then.

After the Revolution of February, 1917, when the Kerensky government came to power, the Russian exiles were able to return home at last. Ehrenburg traveled by way of England, sailing on the same boat as my mother and her family, who had also been political exiles since 1905. The February Revolution had brought a new exhilaration to Russia, but already there was dissension among the political exiles and a feeling of impending trouble as they neared their destination. My mother, then a young girl, remembers Ehrenburg walking around on the ship's deck wrapped in a romantic-looking plaid cape. He was twenty-six years old, a young poet with a measure of recognition. Although the voyage was punctuated by submarine scares, the passengers shared the joys of return; the old regime had fallen at last, they were going home. In his memoirs, Ehrenburg describes an Estonian painter, a friend of his, who was also aboard ship returning to Russia. The man had a French wife who was staying behind. Anxious for his safety, the painter's French mother-in-law had provided him with an inflatable life-saving suit that made him look like an oversized duck. This Estonian painter in his astonishing costume is also part of my childhood lore, for he made a great impression on my mother and her sisters.

The twenties were productive years for Ehrenburg. Besides poetry, he also wrote essays and novels. He acknowledged Pasternak early as a very great poet; he publicly defended his memory last year. In 1922 he edited an anthology of contemporary Russian verse, remarkable in the lasting excellence of his choices. The introductions to the poets, some of whom were little known in 1922, are written in a language which is dated because of a certain "modernistic" style then fashionable, but the acuteness of the judgments is striking. The selections testify to Ehrenburg's understanding of contemporary themes. From Alexander Block, for example, he quotes *The Scythians*, a poem about Russia's position between Europe and the Asiatic world, truer than ever today. The Scythians, the ancient inhabitants of the South of Russia, who symbolize Russia in this poem, invite Europe for the last time to a fraternal banquet. The Scythians address the Old World:

You are but millions—we are an infinite number.
Measure yourselves against us, try.
We are the Scythians, we are the Asians you call us
With slanted and greedy eye.

Centuries of your days are but an hour to us,
Yet like obedient guards
We've held a shield between two hostile races:
Europe, and the Mongol hordes.

Hundreds of years go by, still you look eastward,
Collecting, melting our pearls,
And laughing at us as you wait for the ripe moment
To blast our walls.

But time has come to term and the evil hour
Flaps its wings. Each day multiplies
Offenses; soon of your very Paestum
There will be no trace.

To love the way our blood can love—
Have those long days
Since you forgot the way rendered you blind
To love that burns, destroys?

These we still love: the fever of cold numbers,
The gift of heavenly visions.
And these we know: the piercing Gallic wit,
Germany's somber genius.

And we remember a Paris street's inferno
And the damp freshness of Venice,
The smell of distant lemon groves, and of Cologne
The smoky hugeness.

The flesh, we crave—its taste, its color, heavy
And deadly to the rose.
Is it our crime if your frail skeletons
Crumble in tender paws?

From war and horror come to our open arms,
The embrace of kin,
Put the old sword in its scabbard while there's time,
Hail us as friends.

Lest, at the plains and forests, before the marching
Handful of Europe's men
We step aside, bound by no promise, and show
Our Asian face again.

Yes, come, stream to the Urals where we'll clear
The battle site you'll need
For steel machinery with calculated breath
To meet the horde.

But we, we will no longer shield you
Nor fight at all,
Content observing with our narrow eyes
The death-brew boil.

Nor shall we flinch to see the ferocious Hun
Pillage each corpse,
Herd all his horses into church and burn
Mounds of white flesh.

Ah, Old World, before you have perished, join
Our fraternal banquet. Hear
Perhaps for the last time summoning you
The barbaric lyre!

Julio Jurenito, a novel influenced by the surrealist era, is a satiric attack on bourgeois mentality. It was Ehrenburg's first work in prose and it is now his favorite; he claims that he "found his own voice" there more than anywhere else. It is a highly imaginative, unconventional work. Interestingly, Lenin admired it.

Ehrenburg became inspired by Diego Rivera's tales of his native land and used them as background. Most of his subsequent novels differ from *Julio Jurenito:* they are *romans à thèse* and ought to be read as such. Philip Toynbee, in a recent review of *The Spring*, said: "I suspect that Ehrenburg knows what he is doing. I suspect that he is writing quite deliberately as an educator; that he is sacrificing his own talent for the sake of the future. And if this is the case should we who live in a society where artistic freedom is taken for granted mock or despise his attempts to bring greater freedom to his own country? I don't think we should."

Thus, *The Thaw*, published in 1954, described the atmosphere preceding and immediately following Stalin's end.

The novel raised a storm and was condemned by a congress of writers for "deviationism." This was at a time when the euphoria and confusion caused by Stalin's death had subsided. The government realized that if writers were to speak freely, the Party would lose its hold over them. Slowly, however, Ehrenburg's view of Stalin and the relatively liberal ideas expressed in *The Thaw* have become accepted in the Soviet Union. Considering the years when these ideas were formulated, they are prophetic, or perhaps simply remarkably knowing. The term "thaw" is now used to designate the liberalization which followed Stalin's death.

Ehrenburg personally knew the best poets of his time. Today he speaks enthusiastically of the "era of poetry" in the twenties, contrasting it with the present, which boasts only a "day of poetry." But, Ehrenburg listens to these new voices: Andrei Voznesenski is in his opinion the best among the very young poets. However, his favorites are still, as he calls them, "the five": Pasternak, Mayakovsky, Mandelstam, Tsvetayeva, and Akhmatova. He considers it a personal responsibility to make Mandelstam and Tsvetayeva better known in the Soviet Union.

Osip Mandelstam is about to be published in the USSR for the first time since the thirties. Mandelstam never had much fame, although he was recognized from the start as a poet's poet by lovers of Russian letters. He was born in 1891, the same year as Ehrenburg, a year later than Pasternak. He was an intensely original poet, a member of the acmeist school, as was Akhmatova. The acmeist school was a loosely linked group opposed in spirit to the symbolists. Like the imagists in England and America at that time, they were trying to free verse from the encumbrances of Victorian rhetoric. Osip Mandelstam wrote only four small volumes of hermetic neo-classic poems. Woven into an intricate personal imagery, there is an acute awareness of our epoch in his poems. His works represent one of the highest moments of Russian poetry.

In his memoirs, *People, Years, Life,* Ehrenburg describes Mandelstam as he knew him: "He was small, frail, and he often threw back his head, which was topped by a tuft of red hair. He loved the image of the rooster near the Acropolis tearing the night with his cry, and he himself resembled a young rooster when he recited . . . in his soft bass voice." The rooster, herald of new life, is a recurrent symbol in Mandelstam's poetry. The Crimea, where Mandelstam lived at the height of the Civil War, inspired some of his finest poems. It was in the Crimea that the friendship between Mandelstam and the Ehrenburgs developed.

For years Ehrenburg served as a main link between the Soviet Union and Europe and, more particularly, between French and Communist intellectuals. His unwavering faith in the Communist doctrine saw him through several eras of dangerous political upheavals, but there are indications that at the end of the forties he was threatened with arrest. Despite this he managed to travel during a period of extreme and vindictive isolationism. In post-Stalinist USSR he alone had a wide knowledge of contemporary French affairs. His role in this connection was and still is an important one: he helped keep a small window open to the outside, which could at least benefit the limited world of Communist intellectuals. Today he finds himself with something resembling a monopoly on French cultural affairs: most Soviet contacts with French writers are negotiated through Ilya Ehrenburg.

In his memoirs we recognize the Ilya Ehrenburg of his early writings—a highly cerebral, caustic man so utterly unsentimental as to appear sometimes unfeeling. But in addition to those traits there is something else in the memoirs.

Here Ehrenburg reaches a new dimension: his writing is warmer, freer.

The impact of *People, Years, Life* has been enormous in the Soviet Union. For readers who are his contemporaries Ehrenburg re-creates the atmosphere and the ideas of their youth. The course of his life coincides with that of many Russian intellectuals, and nothing quite so panoramic has yet been written on their place in history. To the younger Soviet reader Ehrenburg opens up an entirely new world of pre-revolutionary struggles, of Montparnasse Bohemia, of modern art. Some of the things that Ehrenburg states on the subject might seem banal to the Western reader—but we must bear in mind that they appear daring and exciting to the less sophisticated young Soviet. One might venture to say that *People, Years, Life* will prove to be the most important book to be published during this decade in the USSR. Ehrenburg is the first writer in Russia to have described the past in a tone relaxed and yet so incisive.

Today, because of the accelerated tempo of our lives, our relationship to the past tends to become ambiguous. We oversimplify and stylize ill-understood events, unfulfilled experiences; we put unpleasant memories out of our minds. This is a natural enough human tendency, but it is particularly strong in Russia, where the fact that history has been rewritten time and again since the twenties has had its effect. We are witnessing the spreading in the USSR of a more candid, comparatively more truthful interpretation of history. The recent revelations about Stalin testify to this.

In contributing to this rehabilitation of the past Ehrenburg has indirectly rehabilitated himself in the eyes of those who might feel that he has betrayed his friends, the tragic Russian writers: Babel, Tsvetayeva, Mandelstam . . . Ehrenburg's memoirs, whether accidentally or in a calculated manner, have definitely encouraged a new Soviet attitude towards the recent past. He speaks of the past faithfully, although he is obviously cautious at times and certain episodes remain fragmentary. Never departing from matter-of-factness, he manages to make the past more real to the Soviet reader. He also describes many foreign countries from which the Soviet citizen, unable to travel, is alienated: Ehrenburg succeeds in making those countries seem less inaccessible and not at all evil.

Most critics find Ehrenburg's *People, Years, Life* an exceptionally interesting literary and human document. But others have questioned his fragmentary approach, and they perhaps remember the ill-fated "Anti-Nazi Jewish Committee." Ehrenburg was the only member not killed by Stalin—and he might have survived, thanks to a violently anti-Zionist article which he published in *Pravda* on October 28, 1948. This article definitely echoed Stalin's policies but it didn't create them, it didn't intensify them, it didn't cause anyone's arrest. As for the incompleteness of the memoirs, Russian cultural affairs are in a state of flux, and to date *People, Years, Life* has been published only partially. In his new-found voice, measured and yet moving, Ehrenburg may tell us many fascinating things yet.

TO LENINGRAD

13 / A Festive Train Ride

A radiance travels the terrifying height
Is it a star there, sighing.
Star of transparency, wandering light
Your twin, Petropolis, is dying.

The dreams of earth catch fire on high,
A green star shimmers, sighing.
O, if you are the star of water and sky
Your twin, Petropolis, is dying.

A monstrous ship on that terrifying height
Spreads out its wings for flying.
In a beautiful poverty, green star of night
Your twin, Petropolis, is dying.

The glass of spring breaks, the wax of immortality
melts down,
On the black Neva lying
O, if you are a star, Petropolis, your town,
Your twin, Petropolis, is dying.
—OSIP MANDELSTAM, "Petropolis' Twin," 1917,
from *Tristia*

Towards the end of February suddenly I began
to feel immensely tired. I woke up one morning in the grayness of my room at the Metropole feeling oppressed. Only

a little wintry light filtered through the heavy curtains. My watch had stopped. From the light it was impossible to tell what time it was. I had gone to bed late the night before and had stayed awake for a long time thinking about the evening I had just spent with close friends of my family, a middle-aged man, his wife, who was a painter, and their son. They had lived for many years as émigrés in France. It was our first reunion since 1947, when we spent a summer vacation together in the Alps. The S.'s son was a few years younger than I. Towards the end of 1947—after several decades of exile—the whole family had been given a visa to return to Russia. This was the euphoric aftermath of the war, when the USSR and the West had come closer together through the common fight against Germany. The S.'s had been heedless of rumors about the increasing harshness in the Soviet regime. Soon after their arrival in the USSR they were arrested and sent to Siberia—without judgment and without apparent cause, for they were quite pro-Communist in their opinions. They were interned in separate work camps while their teen-aged son stayed with relatives. After Stalin's death, the camps were disbanded and the S.'s were free to come back to Moscow.

The evening at their house started out to be a happy one. We shared many recollections: Paris, our lovely summer vacation on Lake Annecy; boating, hiking in the mountains. Then the conversation moved on to present-day Moscow, and I discovered that the S.'s were unusually well-informed about the intellectual life of the city. Mr. S. worked as a translator while Mrs. S. illustrated childrens' books. Their son was attending Moscow University. The S.'s were clearly happy with their lives. They were still the cheerful, united family I had known in France.

Towards the end of the evening, at my insistence, the

S.'s told me a little about the breaking up of the camps at Stalin's death, how the guards vanished and the inmates formed their own government. Mrs. S. spoke of the woman's camp where she spent several years. She said only a few sentences about her experiences but what they evoked was terrifying: the majority of her companions were simple women, overrun by their elemental drives, sexual urges, hysteria. It was possible to survive in this sea of passions only through a great amount of inner strength and self-respect—which Mrs. S. obviously had. Far from feeling that her years in exile were wasted, she was convinced that she had matured morally during that time. The tone with which my friends spoke of their experiences—reluctantly and yet not bitterly—demonstrated that it is quite possible for good people to live through the least deserved, harshest of trials without losing their spirit. There was a certain serenity about the S.'s, although Mrs. S. admitted that she found the hard Moscow winter too long and she was occasionally homesick for Italy, where she had lived as a young girl. The S.'s talked of their sufferings objectively, as though what had happened had no connection with their present lives.

The S.'s apartment was tiny—two small rooms. It was extremely modest but filled with drawings and paintings. Mrs. S.'s artist's materials lay on a small table near the window, and potted green plants were massed all around. The intimate familiar atmosphere made the S.'s tales all the more horrible. They suggested boundless injustice, immense misery, cruel endless Siberian winters, hundreds, thousands, millions of exiles. At the time of my visit to the S.'s, Russians did not speak about concentration camps openly, except to close friends. Now, three years later, we know some of the Soviet statistics about the Stalinist days—fifteen to twenty million Russians killed in purges. Those purges,

which usually affected people in responsible positions—
Party members, civil servants, executives, intellectuals—
created a feeling of fear, a hesitancy to speak or to act in
an independent way which has not yet vanished completely.
It caused untold damage to Soviet society by destroying
much of its elite.

I said good-bye to my hosts trying not to show them
how upset I was. The S.'s lived on the top floor of a dilapidated apartment house in the Arbat, and the staircase was
barely lit, untidy. Stepping onto the snowy sidewalk I burst
into sobs. The street was fortunately deserted. I walked back
to the hotel, following narrow side streets with their small
log houses buried deep in snow. On the way I saw only
ghostly figures of women sweeping the snow off the pavement.

That night my dreams were populated with swarming
disheveled crowds, figures not unlike Neizvestni's crea-
tions.

The next morning, lying in my dark room in the Metropole, I decided that an excursion outside of Moscow was
what I needed: it seemed wise to leave behind for a few days
my absorption with the city, its people and their problems.
They threatened me with exhaustion. I had planned at first
to leave the USSR by way of Leningrad, but it occurred to
me that a separate trip there now would provide a diversion.
I rang the Intourist office from my room and was told that
I could go at whatever time I chose. The idea of taking a
train to Leningrad was tempting. Civilized as the Moscow-
Leningrad run today is, perhaps it would evoke something
of the train rides described in Russian novels and particularly
in *Doctor Zhivago*. I made a reservation for the same evening
on an overnight train, the *Red Arrow*. The Intourist office
saw to it that I was accommodated even though reservations

were difficult to obtain at that time of year. It was the beginning of the three-week winter recess at the University when students from all over the USSR converge on Moscow and Leningrad. As a foreign tourist, however, I even had a choice of sleeping arrangements on the train: I could choose between "hard" and "soft" accommodations, as second and first class are respectively called. It seemed more interesting to meet three Russians on a train rather than just one, and so I chose the least expensive arrangement, a "hard" berth in a compartment for four.

I made several telephone calls canceling my engagements for the following week. Among other friends, I phoned Evtushenko, who said that he also was going to be in Leningrad then. Would I come to a poetry reading which he was giving there? He also told me that George, a poet whom I had met through Evtushenko, was in Leningrad at the time. I was to send a wire to George, said Evtushenko. He would show me around Leningrad. I knew of no one in Leningrad except two very elderly aunts and I followed Evtushenko's suggestion.

My arrangements made, I went back to bed and fell asleep in the gray room. The visions brought about by the previous evening loomed forth again briefly and then receded in my mind. I slept all day. When I awoke, it was time to pack my bag. The train for Leningrad was leaving at eleven o'clock at night. Soon, my cousin would be coming to have dinner with me and escort me to the station. Outside, evening was falling. Above the brick wall of the courtyard I could already see the purplish reflection of the neon signs of the Bolshoi Plaza, which gave a mauve tint to the snow edging on the wall.

We had a copious dinner that night—my cousin was always ravenously hungry, as are all self-respecting students.

For once we ate in the main dining room of the Metropole instead of the more informal and soberly decorated café. This dining room is an extraordinary place, immense and dimly lighted. It has an orchestra near a fountain which has rocks and rushing waterfalls and green ferns, all dramatically lighted. The orchestra plays loud dance tunes out of the thirties with an accelerated tempo. There is a narrow dance floor around the fountain, where a couple occasionally ventures, the boy slightly stiff in his new suit, the girl in a high-necked printed frock. But we saw more elegant couples too, slim girls in tight dresses, their long hair loose, wearing very high heels; and young men with longish hair and narrow trousers—"The last of the *stilyagis**," said my cousin. "We had a lot of them in Moscow for a while after the first great influx of tourists. They have become scarce nowadays." And it was true that I saw only a few throughout my stay, mostly around the big hotels in the center of town. Unlike many visitors, I was never approached by *stilyagis*. Once, when I was having dinner with Eugene Evtushenko and several of his friends in a fashionable Armenian restaurant, we were surrounded by a group of such young men, who had recognized the well-known young poet. Evtushenko ignored them: "They are idle, they are like the skin on the milk of our society," he said after they dispersed. "They play no part in our lives . . ." He pronounced the word *penka*—skin of the milk—with great disgust.

At the railroad station there was all the excitement of European trains, when passengers bound for faraway des-

---

* From the word "style"—they are the style followers. They imitate American mannerisms and clothes (leather jackets, blue jeans, etc.) and tend to behave irresponsibly. They love jazz, chewing gum, whiskey . . .

tinations settle themselves into the sleeping cars. It was just like a railroad station in Paris, with its mixed smell of engines and orange peels. Magazines and sodas were sold from little carts by attendants in white; neatly folded blankets and pillows were distributed by other attendants. The *Red Arrow* is a festive train, it didn't at all suggest the train rides of the time of the Revolution.

The compartments were decorated in Victorian fashion and impeccably clean. The berths one on top of the other on both sides were wide. The compartments were not segregated by sexes. My traveling companions had already arrived and were sitting on the edge of their respective berths. On one upper bunk there was a middle-aged ecclesiastical-looking man. I believe he was a rabbi. He was smiling and shy and wore a thin beard; he remained completely silent and went to sleep as soon as the train left. A young man who looked like a student and had a strong, pleasant face was equally silent on the other upper berth. The third passenger made up for these two with her endless chatter. She was a plump middle-aged woman, well-to-do judging by her clothes. She was tightly corseted, wore a felt hat and a fur coat which she soon took off, folding it neatly. She was so much like her counterparts in Western countries that it seemed to me that I had heard her stories many, many times. She was a widow and worked in the administration of a hospital. She had two married daughters and a younger son who wasn't doing too well in his studies—schools were so strict nowadays. She was going to visit her elder daughter living in Leningrad, who had two babies and had just moved to a new apartment. The young man in the upper berth was visibly exasperated by her loquacity. He turned his reading light off demonstratively and hid his head under his sheet.

Slowly the train started to move. I said good-bye to my

cousin through the window and my eyes followed his boy-ish, hatless figure disappearing among the crowd of people waving good-bye.

Passengers discreetly half undressed under their blankets. The Soviet version of Musak poured into the compartment loud popular music interrupted by broadcasts about Soviet internal affairs. "In Voronej a collective farm has produced a thousand bushels of wheat . . ." Finally the train attendant, a woman with a simple wide face who wore a white kerchief around her head, agreed to turn it off. Then she passed around glasses of strong sweet tea. Outside the double windows of the *Red Arrow* the lights of the suburbs began to fade. The Diesel engine accelerated. One could see stretches of gray snow and of black sky. I got into my berth and fell asleep very quickly. Waking up once or twice in the night, I parted the curtain of the train window which was near my head. All I could distinguish through frozen crystals was an immense white flatness gliding by: our breath had turned into a fantastic frozen jungle covering the windowpanes.

It was still pitch-black when we arrived at Leningrad around eight o'clock in the morning. Just before we reached the station the train attendant brought us glasses of boiling tea which somehow made the wet cold outside seem all the more piercing. Never had I been so cold in all of my stay in Russia. I was delighted to see George's face in the crowd. I had met him once or twice with a group of poets in Moscow and liked his southern spirit. He was from Odessa, a war hero turned poet and a rather good poet too. He was older than Evtushenko—perhaps thirty-five or thirty-six— a short, stocky man, with swift gestures and eyes, a balding head. He was witty, expansive, and punctuated his conversation with innumerable proverbs and limericks from

Odessa—Odessa is the Russian Marseilles. He immediately started telling me about his visit to the Hermitage the day before. He had preferred the Rubenses to anything else there. It seemed right for a person like George to love Rubens. He had been a sailor of the Black Sea and Rubens had painted for people not unlike him, seafaring, full-blooded Dutchmen.

The cold was penetrating. George said that there was a thaw in Leningrad and that this wet iciness was peculiar to a maritime climate. We walked along an endless outdoor quay. Then we reached the overheated station, which was flooded with lights and full of hurrying people. On first impression, they looked more citified, more subdued than the Muscovites.

"You look terribly pale!" said George. "You need sleep," he insisted despite my assurance that I had done little else in the last forty-eight hours. Sleep is the Russian answer to all sorts of ills. "Maybe we'd better postpone going around Leningrad for a day. You are bound to get overexcited when you see the Bronze Horseman for the first time!" He laughed. "I'll call you at your hotel around dinnertime. I am staying at the October with a couple of friends whom you'll find interesting—but sleep first!"

It was true that the humid cold made me feel numb and slightly ill, but I doubted that I could sleep again after my night in the train. I followed George's suggestion, however, and went straight to the hotel to which I was assigned, the European. The ride from the station to the hotel was short. "Nevsky Prospect," said the Intourist cab driver, but all I could see in the foggy darkness was a wide street, gas-lit, very much like a street in Paris. There was no snow left, just a shiny wet pavement.

The hotel was in the agony of early morning awakening. All was still dark and I could barely make out the green Art Nouveau décor of the lobby, entwining leaves and stems and unlit lamps in the form of tulips. The receptionist looked cold and tired, the bellboy yawned, a sleepy-looking maid was feebly waxing the floor.

I was happy to crawl into the enormous feather bed which was set in a deep alcove closed off by a curtain. It was conducive to oblivion, and I was asleep before I fully realized that I had reached the city of Pushkin and of the Russian Revolution, the city of my father's youth . . .

I woke up when the telephone in my room rang. It was eight o'clock in the evening. Outside my window it was completely dark again. I had slept through another full day. I regretted having lost all those valuable hours but I had to admit that George's cure had worked. I felt reborn, warm, a little like someone returning from the realm of the shadows. It was good to hear George's sonorous southern voice on the phone. I was to take a taxi and join him and his friends at the Hotel Astoria for dinner.

I asked the taxi driver to take me on a short ride through foggy streets instead of going directly to the Astoria. I had a glimpse of a long straight quay, a yellowish lamp on the edge of the harbor's waters. I understood at once why Russians often proclaim that Leningrad is the most beautiful city in the world. It is a classical city, a city of space and order. Muffled Moscow has retained the quality of an ancient market place, where many races mingle, where the medieval is just around the corner. By contrast severe Leningrad is overpowering: my first impression had been false, it didn't at all look like Paris, which is all softness, an accumulation of happy architectural innovations and accidents. This was a city willed by one man, and even the fog could not soften the geometric contours of Peter's creation.

I thought of Alexander Block, who has captured St. Petersburg's beauty and its hardness. Lines began singing in my memory:

> *In the late autumn*
> *   The quay white with snow,*
> *Out from the harbor*
> *   The heavy ships go—*

and they leave behind a poor sailor. Abandoned, he is so lonely that he can only lie down in the thin snow and die:

> *Most pure, most tender*
> *   winding sheet,*
> *Wrapped in it, sailor,*
> *   is your sleep sweet?*

This I am told was my grandfather's favorite poem.

Block's poems are part of the Russian consciousness, even that of people not at all literary, because they express an anguish which is peculiar to the Russians of our time. Such an anguish suffuses *Doctor Zhivago* for instance. St. Petersburg permeates Block's writings, but the impact of the city varies; it is sometimes a vague, dreamlike background for his mystical poems, sometimes a concrete city. Block was obsessed with the sense that something fatal and decisive was about to happen to himself, to Russia, to the world.

On a first view, in wintertime, Leningrad looked like the setting for some strange prophetic event. The fog was not the soothing Dickensian fog which gives London its identity. Rather, it was a curtain hiding a predestined city, half threat, half promise. It is remarkable that Russia's most visionary writers, Gogol, Dostoevsky, Block were from St. Petersburg, the least Slavic of all Russian cities.

Block wrote no in-between poems: his unsuccessful work is frankly sentimental and is difficult to read today. But his best poems are more than beautiful. It is said that Block was in a state of trance the night he wrote *The Twelve*, which is about the twelve Red soldiers marching through a fantastic revolutionary Leningrad. In the snow-blown city, through scenes of violence and despair, they are preceded by Christ himself, a promise of salvation. In one night Block gave the Russian Revolution its highest literary expression.

The Hotel Astoria, where we were to have dinner, could have best been described by Block, who was a master at capturing the excitement as well as the coldness of public gathering places, of restaurants, of crowded cafés. The enormous dining hall where I looked for George was filled with people and noise. The Astoria is Leningrad's largest hotel, and its turn-of-the-century decorations made the lobby of the European seem quite sedate. Stained glass, polished stone, gilt, nothing was spared to make it palatial. Built around 1900, it has been kept up lovingly in the same style ever since. It evoked the pre-revolutionary days in Russia, years of safety and prosperity, when wealthy inhabitants of St. Petersburg, unaware of the rising social and political unrest, traveled to Paris every year. No doubt they liked to find at home the same magnificence as abroad. For their pleasure malachite and jade from the Urals were turned into imitations of ponderous French styles. A gallery for musicians ran all around the dining room. It was empty but one could imagine a wave of music rushing down from it, poignant tzigane music dear to the Russians of that era.

I finally found George and his friends settled in a relatively quiet corner of the restaurant. They greeted me with friendliness, then they continued their animated conversation; they were discussing Sergei Eisenstein's famous movie, *Potemkin.* I soon understood that two of George's friends, Alexei and Vladimir, were poets and that the third one, Fedya, was a movie director. Fedya had a reticent attitude at first, as if he was ill-at-ease in this group of uninhibited writers; he was well acquainted only with George. But progressively he lost his reserve, without, however, becoming as exuberant as the poets, who treated me like an old friend from the start. It was extraordinary to be met at once with such directness. The Russian absence of formalities is often commented upon by foreigners with varying degrees of sympathy. There is a certain simple-mindedness in it and it can be disconcerting or irritating or endearing, depending on one's mood.

For the young Russian poets I was an ideal audience: the poetry which absorbed them held an all-important place in my upbringing. As a small child in Le Plessis, I remember being nestled in my father's arms just before bedtime and listening to his flowing, slightly monotonous reading of Pushkin's *The Prophet.* It didn't matter that our neighbors, noisy French factory workers, could sometimes be overheard in the next-door apartment. *The Prophet* seemed to me beautiful, although blurred and obscure to my young mind. The swinging of the verse held me spellbound; Russian poets tend to read poetry with an emphasis on rhythm which gives the reading hypnotic power. In *The Prophet,* Pushkin describes how God invests the prophet, who is really the poet, with divine power. With a sword He opens the poet's breast and takes out his heart and replaces it with a holy fire which the poet will share with his fellow men. Except that in Russian the word "sword" and the word for "rubber ball" sound very much alike. I was persuaded that God opened the poet's breast with a ball. This didn't diminish my pleasure; somehow it made the poem more familiar and quite intelligible. My parents' attitude toward poetry had nothing in common with the cult of art for art's sake fashionable in their youth. Rather, poetry was a moral force, and Pushkin's *The Prophet* is a good expression of it.

The dinner at the Astoria turned out to be a special occasion. Vladimir and Alexei were celebrating; their poems had just appeared in the *Literary Gazette*. This was a great event, especially since the poems selected for publication were lyrical, without political overtone. To appear in the *Gazette*, a biweekly literary newspaper, is an important step in a Soviet poet's career. The real sanction of one's importance, however, is in being accepted by *Pravda*, the official newspaper of the Communist Party, as was recently the case with Evtushenko.

Alexei and Vladimir were friends. Alexei was a handsome man with a bushy mustache. He smoked a pipe. Vladimir was lean, with a lot of wavy dark hair, a bony, intense face. His last name indicated that he was of Georgian origin. He was a little shy, and from the start I felt a special warmth toward him.

It became apparent to me that George, with his open, dynamic character was to some extent the protector of Alexei and Vladimir, both more retiring as people, and lesser known as poets. George was the kind of person who naturally takes over a group—the "soul of society" as the Russians term the "life of the party." He was successful as a movie script writer. With the assistance of Alexei and Vladimir, he was working on a movie about the Soviet Navy in World War II which was then being filmed in Leningrad.

Our meal lasted for several hours. Each of my new friends insisted on ordering something he especially liked and sharing it with the others. We had pickled mushrooms, chicken à la Kiev, beef Stroganoff . . . Then there were many toasts by the poets to one another, to their future, to my first visit to Russia. To be able to partake in the toasting, I resorted to my cognac-and-coffee technique. The poets talked about poetry and the making of the movie, about the intricacies of Soviet publishing. I couldn't follow many of their jokes because they referred to people and events unknown to me. One thing was clear, however: the poets' world was freer and more lively than the painters'. They were in high spirits and their mood was not just the result of the gaiety of this meeting.

At the end of the dinner there was a surprise: Fedya had a car. This was by no means common among the young Russians I knew, although several of my painter friends in Moscow shared an old automobile. I was to be taken on a night ride around Leningrad.

The blanket of fog which hid the city until then was vanishing. The night was still cold and humid, but it was suddenly full of thousands of yellow lights. Necklaces of distant street lamps revealed classic façades. We slowly drove down the Nevsky Prospect, deserted at that hour. We reached the Neva, and to our right stood the Winter Palace, huge and yet graceful. In front of us was an immense, very slightly arched bridge. Halfway across it stood four columns, their shafts decorated with huge bronze ships' prows. The city was like a frigid Venice—a Venice spread out and frozen. We drove across the square which lies in front of the Winter Palace, a cobblestone expanse broken only by the granite column erected to the memory of Alexander I and topped by a somber angel brandishing a cross.

Rastrelli's exquisite baroque architecture slowly unfolded before our eyes. The Winter Palace was painted a pale blue; it had white stucco columns framing tall ornate windows. Dark statues in seeming disarray stood on its roof. Opposite it, the endless façade of another massive palace was relieved only by a broad arched gate through which the Soviet militia streamed in October of 1917 on its way to the Winter Palace, where the doomed Provisional Government was encamped.

We drove to the end of the plaza and into the dark streets between palaces—several stand there: the Hermitage, the Marble Palace, the Grand Ducal palaces. As in Venice, a footbridge curved over a narrow canal, leading to a sculptured eighteenth-century doorway. Through side streets we drove around and between palaces; then we reached the quay over the wide dark river. The river was in movement, here and there the thaw had broken up the ice. The scraping of chunks of ice against each other made a soft noise. The element of water was to be felt everywhere: in the cold moist air, in the sound of the river, in the profusion of marine motifs decorating the buildings; stucco ropes and fish scales, anchors and mermaids faintly visible in the light of gas lamps. Across the Neva, the other shore outlined by street lights seemed infinitely far away. The vista was perfectly harmonious, combining an Italian gracefulness with classical rigidity.

Slowly, we followed the quay. The domed buildings across the river became more distinct. The Fortress of Peter and Paul was pointed out to me, a dark mass almost lost in the river mist. We were nearing the small square adjoining the quay where the Bronze Horseman stands. There he was, on our left, leaping into nothingness, the enormous man on the enormous horse, black against the unmelted snow on the lawn. Heaviness and a kind of weightlessness are united in this statue of Peter the Great, just as in Peter himself two opposite tendencies were joined: Russian primitiveness and an acute intuition of the new age. The empty eyes looked high over the river, toward the spire of St. Peter and St. Paul. The upraised petrified face gave a feeling of energy, of will arrested in time. Everything around us was quiet, except for the roaring of a distant automobile engine. A segment of the quay was being repaired in that spot. We sat in silence on a pile of granite blocks. The stones must have come from far away, as there are no quarries near Leningrad. The city was built on marshes, and in the time of Peter all vessels entering the harbor of St. Petersburg were required to bring several large stones in their cargo to help build the new city. We looked for a long time at the statue—a homage of Catherine the Great to Peter, her name carved in bigger letters than his on the assymetrical granite base. Then we looked towards the famous Senate Square beyond it. There in 1825, for the first time in Russian history, the Czars' power was challenged by the Decembrists.

14 / City of the Past

Return to my city, dearer to me than tears,
To its veins, the swollen throat of childhood nights,
Return, remembering . . . swallow, o quickly then
The codliver oil of Leningrad's rivered lights.

Recognize swiftly that small day of December—
See, in the sinister asphalt, eggyolks run!
St. Petersburg, say that I need not die yet.
You still list the number of my telephone.

St. Petersburg! I have kept all your addresses
That I may find the voices of the dead.
I live on a black stairway; against my temple
A constant doorbell strikes, tearing the flesh.

And all night long I await the sound of callers
Shifting the heavy handcuffs of the door.
                              —OSIP MANDELSTAM, "Leningrad," 1930

At night, Leningrad was the most romantic of
cities. Here, as in Venice, it is easy to imagine shadowy figures lost in the distance. In the daytime the city remains
dark and foggy; the fog had a yellowish tint and "lemon
yellow" is often used in descriptions of wintry Leningrad.
The sun seldom shone there, but when it did, I understood

for the first time Osip Mandelstam's image of Petropolis' twin dying. For a fleeting moment the city's monuments were reflected in the waters of the Neva, the Winter Palace was a double fairy castle. Its aqua blue façade was reflected in the water and the floating ice, and it gave the ice a brilliant blue hue. But this vision faded at once, the sun disappeared behind a dense cloud, Leningrad took on the sadness of an ice-bound seaport, shrouded in a fog yellowed by city fumes.

A friend of mine from New York, a passionate art lover, had warned me about the shortness of winter days in Leningrad. I had to organize my time around the scarcity of daylight because the Hermitage is lacking in artificial lighting. After a breakfast of caviar or smoked salmon I would take the tram on the Nevsky Prospect down to the Hermitage. The entrance of the museum was already swarming with young people. They were mostly students visiting Leningrad during the mid-year holidays. The cloakroom had long lines of restless adolescents, who were gay and noisy. My heart sank at the thought of having to share the art works with so much youthful enthusiasm, but once the students left the cloakrooms and proceeded to the exhibition halls they were on their best behavior. Starry-eyed, often holding hands, they went from room to room in perfect silence. The younger ones circulated in orderly rows led by a female museum guide. These guides were scholarly-looking women: flat shoes, no make-up, hair neatly drawn back. In practiced voices they lectured about the paintings on view. What they had to say sounded sensible and dull and seemed without any noticeable Marxist slant.

The Hermitage, which has the reputation of being one of the best museums in Europe, lived up to my expectations: it was an endless source of enjoyment. I looked at the famous Scythian gold ornaments, which I had wanted to see ever since I read André Malraux's description of the art of the steppes in *The Voices of Silence*. They were collected by the Czars long before anything at all was known about the origin of these gold and bronze jewels found in burial mounds in the great plains of the south-west of Russia. They constitute one of the great treasures of the Hermitage. At George's recommendation, I allowed sufficient time for the Rubenses, which indeed were many and overwhelmingly luxurious. A certain sentimentality in taste during the nineteenth century made the Dutch painters immensely popular in Russia: the numerous Rembrandts to be found at the Hermitage represent the more intimate aspect of the Dutch master—a domestic-looking young Virgin with a child in a crib, a homely Danaë under a shower of gold. There are also many rooms of minor Dutch works, with surprises once in a while. Thus at the end of a long corridor, in an unlit doorway, I discovered accidentally a Breughel: in the middle of an open field, three ferocious-looking soldiers were about to attack a family of peasants, numb with fear. It was a somber painting, a window into a threatening world, all the more forceful because of its inconspicuous yet dramatic location.

I had another haunting encounter in a Leningrad museum. In the Museum of Russian Art I unexpectedly came across a plaster cast of Peter the Great's face taken by Carlo Rastrelli, the Italian father of the architect who built the Winter Palace. It had been made during the Czar's lifetime. Fittingly, it stood in a doorway separating a room of icons from a hall of eighteenth-century paintings. Those were mundane portraits, imitations of Western styles which were brought to Russia through Peter's efforts to eradicate the Byzantine art of old Russia. It came to my mind that this

cast had served as a model for Falconnet's statue, standing
on the bank of the Neva, but whereas the head of the Bronze
Horseman is stylized, Rastrelli's cast has a frightening life-
like wildness. Peter had had a low brow, large wide-set eyes,
a flattened jaw, a savage face. Even the shimmering icons in
the next room faded in contrast with this image reflecting
the inhuman determination that went into the building of
modern Russia.

I remember looking at an exhibit of Piranese prints in a
long, grand hall in the Hermitage, high above the half-
frozen Neva. The tarnished gilt on the woodwork, the per-
vading musky smell spoke of faded royal splendor. Outside,
the light was pale, wintry, the river was all yellowish ice and
black water, moving very slowly with that monotonous
scraping sound which I had noticed on my first evening in
Leningrad. Piranese's Roman ruins evoked a glorious past
and a gentle implacable decay—a decay which will ulti-
mately engulf even St. Petersburg. Heavily damaged during
the siege in World War II, when half of its population died
of starvation, the city has been painstakingly reconstructed
in accordance with eighteenth- and early nineteenth-century plans. It is one of the most integrated architectural ensembles in existence today, a credit to Soviet scholarship and
good taste. And yet, subjectively, I felt that Leningrad was
a dead city. I found myself trying to imagine it as it was at
the turn of the century. Around that time, my grandfather,
a promising young writer originally from Orel, a middle-
sized provincial town of central Russia, moved from Moscow to St. Petersburg. St. Petersburg was considered more
fashionable and intellectually more advanced than Moscow.
It was the city of the Russian symbolist school—with which
Andreyev was in sympathy—but a tasteless germanic family lived in the Winter Palace. Nicholas II was the absolute

ruler of Russia—a mediocre man unequal to the events about to unfold. The lovely baroque buildings of St. Petersburg were painted a Victorian oxblood red. The Imperial capital was a place of wealth and pomp. It was also a city of revolutionary ferment under tight police patrol. Dostoevsky had died not too long before, and Alexander Block still haunted the desolate workers' quarters. A great friendship blossomed between Leonid Andreyev and Maxim Gorki— then it faded as their views and their personalities diverged. Andreyev, weighed down by dark premonitions, darker even than Block's, withdrew into loneliness. The February Revolution broke out as my father was finishing his studies at the gymnasium in St. Petersburg; mobs of people milled through the streets for days and days. There were high hopes, but deserters in increasing numbers came to St. Petersburg, foretelling trouble. . . .

St. Petersburg became Leningrad after the Revolution. It suffered greatly in the post-revolutionary years, and in the thirties it witnessed many persecutions, those of intellectuals in particular.

Later, war bled the city; the older people who live there now are dignified and profoundly sad, judging by those I came to know. Life goes on in Leningrad, but for a visitor like myself it seems primarily a relic of the past—a very recent past, one which has contributed to the shaping of the twentieth century, but nonetheless a past irrevocably gone.

Despite its melancholy, Leningrad was to me a fascinating city. The pleasure of looking at painting was almost always succeeded by poetry readings at night. My evenings were spent in the company of the poets. By seven o'clock the poets were finished with their work at the studio and ready to sit down to a good meal. They were well paid for their work on the movie and could afford the best restaurants. I had many tourist coupons saved up and could also indulge in luxury. Once, my friends came to have dinner at the European, but this was not our most successful evening. When we sat in one of the lounges after dinner laughing and talking there was visible consternation among the hotel employees. The European was like an old-fashioned, conservative hotel anywhere in the West—it was simply not adaptable to public gaiety.

My room at the European opened on a side street linking the Nevsky Prospect to a public garden dominated by Alexander Pushkin's statue. Behind the statue, the Russian Museum spread its classical columns. If I unlatched the hinged pane of the double window and leaned out, I could see Pushkin, a large bronze figure extending his hand. I had the feeling he was greeting me with a welcoming gesture. At closer range, one could see that it was a rather heavy, realistic statue and Pushkin's features looked quite African.

It is strange to think that a mixture of African and Russian blood gave Russia its greatest poet. Pushkin had a Negro grandfather, a certain Hannibal, given to Peter the Great as a slave. Hannibal became a favorite of Peter, who educated and ennobled him.

Pushkin's voice has rarely resounded truly in English: his poetry has proved to be almost untranslatable. How trying it must be for foreigners to be forever enthusiastically told of Pushkin's greatness!

One evening, Vladimir, Alexei, and I went out for a walk to look at Pushkin's statue by moonlight. Having brushed the snow off a bench, we sat near the black statue, the raised hand stretched high above our heads. The poets recited excerpts from Pushkin's verse. Even I, with my bad memory, could quote passages from favorite poems. Then

Alexei read out loud the lines engraved at the base of the statue. Pushkin's *Exegi Monumentum* ends as follows:

> *. . . And to the people long shall I be dear*
> *Because kind feelings did my lyre extoll*
> *Invoking freedom in an age of fear*
> *And mercy on the broken soul.**

A silence fell. I noticed that Alexei and Vladimir looked at each other somewhat wearily. Alexei sighed, he turned away. When I asked him what it was that made him sad, he answered with these lines from one of his own poems, which I quote from memory:

> *We may gather rhymes, long or short ones,*
> *Any we like—*
> *No one will summon us to the Senate Square.*
> *Nor in heavy carriages through the snow*
> *Will true women follow us now.*

—a reference to the wives of the Decembrists, who went into Siberian exile with their husbands. I didn't press Alexei, but I knew he felt that freedom as Pushkin had dreamt it hadn't come yet; in the meantime, the exalted spirit of the Revolution had died.

This evening witnessed a complete change of humor on Alexei's part; as we went to the Astoria for dinner he revealed a satirical side. George could not join us and Alexei and Vladimir were somehow more relaxed when the outgoing George was not there. We were early and the enormous dining room was still empty; its ornate décor looked weird and gaudy without the crowds of people which com-

---

* This translation is by Vladimir Nabokov, who is one of the more successful translators of Pushkin. His rendering of the short drama in verse *Mozart and Salieri* is particularly readable.

plemented it during dinner hours. There were several alcoves off the main hall. Some were shaped like huge flowers
and contained only one table, while larger ones served as
separate small dining rooms. Their entryways were all
gilded and draped in tasseled velvet. Across the hall from
where we sat, a wedding party was dining in one of the
larger alcoves. The red curtains and the emptiness of the
restaurant made it look exactly like a stage setting. The bride
was very fat and blond, her hair curled and beribboned. The
groom was gauche and diminutive; the mother of the bride
was all dressed up in purple velvet. The whole thing was a
comic sight, and a perfect replica of the hilarious wedding
scene in Mayakovsky's play *The Bed Bug* written in 1928
which depicts not without a touch of sympathy the pre-
revolutionary bourgeois way of life.

Soon, Alexei started to imitate the various members of
the wedding, who were blissfully unaware of the entertain-
ment they were generating. Jokes and puns succeeded each
other in subdued tones. Then Vladimir and Alexei composed mottoes to commemorate the happy event. Alexei explained that these were inspired by the newest socialistic
achievement called the Palace of Matrimony—or some such
name—which was about to open in Moscow. This was
planned as a sort of supermarket where everything necessary for a happy wedding would be made available to the
newlyweds—from a marriage license to bouquets and champagne. Of course the religious ceremony was excluded. I
doubt very much that this "palace," is actually decorated
with funny or even obscene mottoes printed on red
banderoles as Alexei would have it; but he captured to perfection the practical, communistic spirit of such an institution and also its bourgeois overtone. Vladimir and I were
choking with laughter while Alexei, straight-faced, went on

and on in a quiet voice. We had to plead with him to stop when our waiter began looking at us with curiosity, then with indignation.

Alexei could be very bitter at times. When the future of the Soviet Union was discussed, however, he was willing to concede that things had improved in a spectacular manner in the past five years and that they continued to improve not only as far as material life was concerned, but intellectually as well. In his opinion, Ekaterina Furtseva, the Secretary to Soviet Cultural Affairs, was a good influence: liberty in the arts was slowly increasing. However, there was a daily struggle against reactionary traditions within the Writers' Union for those who, like my three friends, were members of the Union.

The poets asked me all sorts of questions about the West. Material conditions didn't particularly interest them, but they were eager to find out about the literary life: they had heard about beatniks. Who were beatniks? Did they have any social ideals? Who were the best French authors today? What was translated out of Soviet literature? Who were my favorite American poets? I was impressed by how much they actually knew about Western affairs. None of them had ever been outside Russia.

After dinner we always went to the October Hotel where the poets stayed. It was located across the way from the main Leningrad railroad station in a commercial section of the city. It was immense and always full of people. In contrast with the European and the Astoria, it was a proletarian hotel, commemorating the October Revolution as its name indicates. It had a big red neon sign on the outside. In the lobby, murals depicted the Soviets taking the Winter Palace in October of 1917. The center of the lobby was occupied by a statue of Lenin, stretching out his arm, in that pose which signifies in the Soviet Union: Lenin-in-October. The elevators were quite small and rickety and people didn't hesitate to push to get in first. It was easier to walk up to the large room which the poets shared on the third floor. The Soviet rule, which doesn't allow a visitor in any room after midnight, wasn't enforced too strictly at the October.* Besides, the poets were friendly with the "floor attendant," a woman who sits at a desk on every floor of a Soviet hotel to assist the guests and also to keep an eye on them. Thus the floor attendant tolerated me, and I spent several unforgettable evenings of poetry reading and conversation in the dimly lit, warm room at the October. It was a shabby room but extremely cozy, with its round table and deep horsehair couch. We sat up late into the night, drinking vodka and tea. The floor attendant provided a kettle of boiling water for brewing fresh tea. Sometimes other poets—natives of Leningrad—joined my three friends. Everyone was very friendly on the surface but when professional questions were discussed I could sense that there was a certain rivalry between the two groups. At the turn of the century Leningrad was the leading cultural center—or so it seemed then.† The rivalry between Moscow and St. Petersburg was an impor-

---

* This rule filled Sholokhov with rage. He told me how once, during the war, he raised a storm in a Moscow hotel where a major's wife wasn't allowed to spend the night with her husband because she wasn't herself registered in the hotel.

† Here is a passage out of Andreyev's journal, 1918: "Moscow . . . in my first years of writing was too rich in its smells, in its everyday life. One couldn't write *Black Masks* there . . . In Moscow, symbolism seemed a passing fashion which might go away like the measles. The nearness of St. Petersburg, which I respect and love sometimes with passion, was good for me. Only after having seen Rome did I have a passing doubt—there is a kinship between Moscow and Rome. What if I was mistaken and true symbolism dwells in the Arbat, and St. Petersburg is thin-blooded, affected? But I had my own, vague beautiful notion of the city."

tant aspect of Russian literary life. In the end Moscow produced more than its share of great writers—Anton Chekhov, Ivan Bunin, Alexei Remizov, Marina Tsvetayeva—and after the Revolution Moscow became the political capital of the USSR and also the cultural leader.

Eugene Evtushenko spent an evening with us at the October. He arrived one night around nine o'clock, exhausted after his public appearance. A button was missing from his coat, where an admiring young girl had pulled it off in her excess of emotion. Evtushenko was slightly annoyed at us for not attending his reading. However, knowing that the Writers' Club, where the reading was to take place, would be mobbed, we had prudently stayed away.

Evtushenko's good mood was soon restored. A button was found to replace the missing one and I was made to sew it on. Evtushenko ordered champagne to drink to Pushkin since we were in the poet's city. He draped himself in his overcoat in a romantic fashion, reading a poem dedicated to Pushkin, and managing somehow to look like him, although Pushkin had been short and dark while Evtushenko is tall and has ash-blond hair.

Afterwards, George and Alexei read their poems. George's were deeply marked by war, strongly cadenced and reminiscent of Tsvetayeva. Alexei's were more subtle, more lyrical: Alexei is an excellent poet, the best in the group in my opinion. As for Vladimir, he was a little reluctant at first. Eventually, he was coaxed into singing his own songs, for he was a composer as well as a poet. I had never heard anything like them, except perhaps for the songs of the French singer, Georges Brassens, who also puts his own incisive but poetic words to music. Vladimir's songs were about Moscow at night, about love, and the simple Russian people and their sufferings. He had a guitar and he accompanied himself as he sang. He was transfigured then, acquiring that handsomeness for which Georgians are famed. I understand that his songs have recently become extremely popular in Moscow. At that time, he had just started composing them and we were virtually his first audience.

All too soon, my stay in Leningrad came to an end. I didn't want to go, but I had to get back to Moscow because my visa was almost up. The Red Arrow was scheduled to leave around ten o'clock one evening. I stopped at the October Hotel on my way to the station to say good-bye to the poets. They were going back to Moscow within a few days too, and I would see them again before leaving the Soviet Union, so it wasn't a final farewell. At the last moment George made an enormous sandwich for me to take on the train—brown bread and garlic sausage. Vladimir agreed to sing a last song, but time was running out. George grabbed my bag and we ran across the street to the railroad station. I jumped into the departing train with hardly enough time for a "thank you" to George for all his kindness. The sandwich was smelly and earned me the disgusted looks of my fellow passengers. But I went on eating it, thinking about George, Alexei and Vladimir and the hours we had spent in their room at the October.

15 / The Dark Russian Nineteenth Century

*. . . And if we, Russians, who live so closely to-
gether in constant misery, understand one another
so poorly that we mercilessly put to death those who
should be pitied or even rewarded, and reward those
who should be punished by contempt and anger—
how much more difficult is it for you Americans to
understand distant Russia? But then, it is as difficult
for us Russians to understand distant America, of
which we dream in our youth and over which we
ponder deeply in our years of maturity. The Jewish
massacres and famine; a Parliament and executions;
pillage and the greatest heroism; the "Black Hundred" and Leo Tolstoi—what a mixture of figures
and conceptions, what a fruitful source for all kinds
of misunderstandings!*

–LEONID ANDREYEV, from a preface to
The Seven Who Were Hanged

One aspect of Leningrad did not reveal itself to
me fully until the end of my visit. When I went on a tour of
the Fortress of St. Peter and St. Paul across the Neva one icy

afternoon just before I left, a new picture of Leningrad's past became clear to me. Until then, this past had been only occasionally brought up, during the course of walks and conversations, by the poet Alexei in particular. Alexei was a student of the various revolutionary movements in Russia. He wanted to know about my mother's family which had three generations in succession fighting against the Czars— they had been liberals, then terrorists, then socialists.

In intensity, the few hours I spent in the fortress compare only with my afternoon with Boris Pasternak, during which the poet told me of his new plays. All at once, I understood why my family is so proud of its revolutionary past. The key to a "Russian consciousness" is there: in having known a secure, gracious existence and in having forsaken it in the name of justice at the risk of ending one's life inside the walls of the Petropavlovskaya, as the Fortress of St. Peter and St. Paul is called in Russian.

The fortress is as omnipresent in Leningrad as the River Neva itself. From almost anywhere in the city one can see its golden spire, its gray walls rising slightly above the vast estuary. Nowadays the Petropavlovskaya is a museum. One wishes that all the obscure, undeserved sufferings, all the anonymous oppressions of yesterday and today could leave behind a monument as laconic and as moving as this fortress.

Tours of the fortress leave from the Cathedral of St. Peter and St. Paul every hour or so. I went there on a clear day, and the golden spire of the church shone against the luminous midafternoon sky. Beyond the low fortress embankments, the river sparkled with a mixture of ice and water. A small crowd was already gathered when I arrived. It was a good sampling: there was a burly old peasant and his wife, a young factory worker with his overcoat tightly belted, and a couple of students eager and curious. Soon our guide appeared, bundled to the ears. She warned us that the fortress was unbearably cold. She was a young woman with an intelligent face and a soft cultivated voice. (I have found that for an outsider like myself, Russian voices reveal not so much a person's education, as his political attitude. Young militant Communists seem to have overly articulated intonations; they often sound like didactic teachers.)

The fortress was built by Peter the Great before the construction of St. Petersburg itself was begun, to protect Russia from Sweden. It was destined to open Russia to European commerce and insure the safety of the harbor. The fortress was erected on a small low island in the estuary of the Neva, in the middle of a complete wilderness. Over a period of several years, Peter used forced labor—soldiers and convicts—to build it. The fortress, however, did not serve its military function. In the eighteenth century, Swedish power declined and the fortress was turned into a prison. It became a place of confinement and execution for innumerable political prisoners.

Peter was first to initiate a tradition of violence at the Petropavlovskaya. He partook personally in interrogations and tortures within its walls. His fits of tyranny were merciless. He exterminated all those who opposed his ideas—members of his family, nobility, clergy. He hated the old Russian customs and particularly Russian religiosity, he despised the Russian lack of practical sense, and he was determined to make a modern nation out of Russia. He married off his nieces to German princes. As a result of those alliances, the Russian Empire was ruled by German, or half-German, or German-educated monarchs throughout the eighteenth and nineteenth centuries. It was at this time that the Slavic tongue was provided with a stiff grammar German in spirit. As a child, I remember the writer Alexei Remizov deploring this fact; I found Russian grammar very complicated and shared his feeling. Everything German was popular with the Czars: German military institutions, German protocol, German ladies-in-waiting, German teachers. Russian writers of that time reacted against this influence. A certain ponderous German individual is recurrent in many works of fiction, notably Dostoevsky's; (the Czarist government was, of course, actively anti-Semitic, but few Jewish caricatures appear in the literature of the period).

We started our tour with a survey of the Cathedral of St. Peter and St. Paul, the official church of the Emperors; from its pulpit anathema was cast on the enemies of the government—such as Emilian Pugatchev, who led a powerful uprising against Catherine the Great, or Count Leo Tolstoi, for his heretical religious and social ideas. Peter intended the spire of his church to dominate all the buildings of the new city. It is an exact replica of a Lutheran church of that time, with its large windows on each side of the church, letting in a double flow of colorless light—no stained glass warms this severe establishment. It gives a feeling of infinite coldness. In the Kremlin, the mixture of holiness and barbarism is indigenous and has a passionate grandeur. In the Cathedral of St. Peter and St. Paul, religion is clearly a tool to enforce and safeguard the power of the Czar.

Wrapping our coats around us as best we could and tightening our mufflers, we left the cathedral for a walk through the Petropavlovskaya's lugubrious casemates and bastions, where generations of Russians were tortured and put to death. There was something abject in the proximity of the church to the prisons—just a few steps across a courtyard.

First, we saw the cells in which the Decembrists were held: their idealistic and yet impractical attempt to give a constitution to Russia had been crushed. Many were executed in the courtyard of the fortress, others were condemned to forced labor in the mines of Siberia. Still others were detained in the Petropavlovskaya, in complete isolation, surrounded by vermin, without the permission to read or write.

Then we were shown the corner in which, at a later date, Dostoevsky had spent eight months awaiting the mock execution which affected him so deeply. Here in this dark hole, Vera Figner, who had been a friend of my maternal grandmother, was imprisoned. She was a member of the terrorist group which called itself the Will of the People. It was formed in an attempt to check through violence the increasing autocracy of the Czars, and it succeeded in killing the Czar Alexander II in 1881. Subsequently, the government's powerful spy system uncovered the Will of the People. Many of its members, altruistic, often puritanical young intellectuals, were executed or shut up in the Petropavlovskaya. Such was the fate of my grandmother's elder brother, Vassily Sukhomlin, who spent several years in the fortress.

Shivering with cold, we followed our guide through hallways opening into dark cells. She was telling us of the regime in the fortress—starvation, cold, torture. She explained how the prisoners managed to communicate with each other by tapping on the walls in code, although this was prohibited and those caught were cruelly punished. One of the Decembrists caused this system of communication to fail in the eighteen-thirties because he didn't know the order of the Russian alphabet, on which the code rested. Like so many Russian aristocrats of his day, he knew French better than Russian. In general, however, the system worked per-fectly and prisoners were even able to lecture to each other on various scholarly subjects.

The heavy silence reigning in the fortress was one of the worst tortures for the inmates, who were literally buried alive behind thick walls, enormous bolted wooden doors. When they died, they were interred anonymously, or dumped in the Neva at night so as not to alarm public opinion with the news of their deaths. I was thinking of my grandfather's story, *The Seven Who Were Hanged*. Never until that afternoon had his novella taken on its full gruesome meaning for me.

The Petropavlovskaya was a formidable prison: no one ever escaped from it and only one person was released as the result of the pressure of public opinion—Maxim Gorki, who spent a month there after the Revolution of 1905. The fortress was run in a methodical German manner. Never-theless, one man came near escaping from the Petropavlov-skaya. His story may be partially familiar to western readers because one of the characters in Dostoevsky's *The Possessed* is modeled after him.

Sergei Nechaev was a young man of modest origin who was active in underground revolutionary work. He had taken part in students' riots in 1869 and had escaped to Switzerland, where he contacted Mikhail Bakunin, the émigré dean of Russian anarchists who lived there in exile. He convinced Bakunin that he was a representative of a vast secret society—the Central Revolutionary Committee—which existed only in his imagination. He gained Bakunin's confidence and his backing. Then he returned to Russia and organized a group called Popular Reprisal, whose principles were profoundly nihilistic. For example, it advo-cated a complete identification of its members with the

"Savage World of Bandits, the Only True Revolutionaries in Russia." Crime was widespread in Czarist Russia, and there were countless runaway soldiers, escaped convicts, former serfs roaming through the country.

Popular Reprisal was run like a secret society. Its members were anonymous and Nechaev's power over them was immense. When one of the nihilists refused to obey Nechaev's orders, he was killed by co-plotters who were all made to participate in the crime. Nechaev wanted them to be linked by common guilt—a "blood tie" which would insure their fidelity to Popular Reprisal. This particular murder served as the point of departure for *The Possessed*. The murder was uncovered and Nechaev fled again to Switzerland, but the Czarist government managed to bring about his extradition on the grounds of murder, a common-law offense. Nechaev was condemned to twenty years of forced labor. Aware of his fanaticism, the Czar Alexander II personally ordered him to be detained in the Petropavlovskaya until his death. Nechaev was put in the "Secret House," the innermost prison of the Petropavlovskaya. At the Petropavlovskaya, everyone—jailers, guards, soldiers—spied on each other, bribed by the police: thus not only Nechaev, but his jailers were under constant police supervision.

Years and years of solitary confinement went by for Nechaev. He was chained at all times and was refused books and writing paper. Yet his devotion to revolutionary ideas did not wane. Slowly he elaborated a plan of escape. He decided to propagandize his guards—seemingly an impossible task, since they were all informing on each other to the authorities. However, on the rare occasions when a guard or a soldier came alone to his cell, Nechaev went into passionate speeches about the miserable fate of the Russian people under the Czars, about the proximity of a revolution, the ultimate sharing of land among the people. Those were ideas which couldn't help moving a lower-class Russian of that time. Nechaev proceeded soberly, yet he must have possessed a singular magnetic power. Within a few years the whole garrison of the Secret House was under his spell. Its every member became deeply involved in revolutionary activity.

Through the intermediary of soldiers, Nechaev established contacts with the outside world, an unprecedented feat in the history of the fortress. He got in touch with the terrorists from the Will of the People. The executive committee of the Will of the People was prepared to assist Nechaev in his plans to escape along a water pipe running outside the fortress down to the Neva. However, their first aim was the assassination of Alexander II. The Will of the People left it to Nechaev himself to decide which was to come first—his escape or the killing of the Czar. Although he had no doubt of his own importance as a revolutionist, Nechaev conceded that Alexander II was to be murdered first. The Czar was killed on March 1st, 1881—the famous First of March of Russian revolutionary history.

This assassination resulted in a tightening of the regime inside the fortress. To its horror, the government realized that certain links existed between the terrorists and the inmates of the Petropavlovskaya, although the exact nature of those links was never discovered. Moved to new quarters in the Secret House, Nechaev continued to spread revolutionary ideas among the guards and to plan his escape. Imprudently, he confided in a certain Mirsky, a convict in the cell next to him. Mirsky, who was not a revolutionary, denounced Nechaev in the hope of gaining his own freedom. All those connected with Nechaev's plans of escape were arrested, including the whole garrison of the Secret House, a total of sixty-nine people. As for Nechaev, he died as a result of intensified brutalities shortly afterwards. Mirsky, however, left the Secret House for forced labor in Siberia— an unprecedented easing of penalty. No revolutionary was ever freed from the Secret House. Boris Pasternak described the obscurity and the glory of the revolutionaries of that period in an epic poem, *1905:*

> *The drums' throbbing is drowned in the roar of the railroad,*
> *The scraping of wheels on the executioner's cart*
> *Drowns in the sharp harangue from the speaker's platform:*
> *Russia, the Land of Serfs, acclaims its reforms!*
>
> *By the prison gate, this is the Will of the People—*
> *Pince-nezed students, Nihilists clad for work.*
> *The tales of our fathers sound like reigns of the Stuarts,*
> *Further away than Pushkin, the figures of dreams.*
>
> *Here Dostoevsky came, and the faithful women.*
> *Who thought that each arrest would yield us a relic?*
> *Rather, they met their deaths assuming oblivion:*
> *Nechaev, underground-dweller, buried them deep.*
>
> *Ah, were it yesterday, thirty years past, and, strolling,*
> *I'd lit that door with my flickering kerosene,*
> *The young girls bent in the dark there, warrior-chemists*
> *With their bombs, would be my mother and her friends.*

BORIS PASTERNAK

Portrait of a Poet

16 / A Walk in Peredelkino

Smoke he'd compared to Laocoon
        And sung the cemetery thistle
And filled the world with a carillon
        Of stanzas ringing in new air,
And a star, clairvoyant of the dark's castle
        Rewarded him with eternal birth
That with all men to come he'd share
        His heritage, the earth.
        —ANNA AKHMATOVA, from "Boris Pasternak," 1936

I hadn't yet undertaken any steps towards arranging an interview with Boris Pasternak. To meet him was my greatest desire and my principal reason for taking on the *Paris Review* assignment, but I wanted to find out first whether for Pasternak's sake it was wise for a foreigner to visit him. In Moscow, opinions were divided on this subject.

The consensus, however, was that there was no reason *not* to call on Pasternak. At worst, he would refuse to receive me.

I had messages and small presents to take to him from my parents and from other admirers. But how to get in touch with him? I soon learned that Pasternak had no phone. I dismissed the thought of writing a note because I feared that he might have some sort of standard rejection form for requests to visit him. My only choice then was to go directly to his house, but it took great effort to bring myself to call unannounced on a man so famous. I was, moreover, afraid that Pasternak in later years would not live up to my image of him suggested by his poems—lyric, impulsive, above all youthful.

My parents had mentioned that prior to being awarded the Nobel Prize, Pasternak held open house on Sundays. (This as a matter of fact seems to be a tradition among Russian writers, and it extends to Russians abroad.) On my third Sunday in Moscow I decided to call on Pasternak at his home in Peredelkino. It was a radiant day and the center of Moscow looked like a dream of the winter city. The streets were full of sightseers—out-of-town families bundled in peasant-like fashion walking towards the Kremlin with faces full of expectation. Their festive air was accentuated by the fresh mimosa many carried, sometimes only a single spray. On Sundays in wintertime large shipments of mimosa come to Moscow. Russians buy it to present to each other or perhaps simply to carry around as if to mark the solemnity of the day.

I decided to take a taxicab to Peredelkino, although I knew of an electric train which went from the Kiev railroad station near the outskirts of Moscow. I was suddenly in a great hurry to get there.

The taxi driver, a youngish man with the anonymous air of taxi drivers everywhere, assured me that he knew the way to Peredelkino which was about thirty kilometers out of town on the Kiev highway. He seemed to find it completely natural that I should want to drive out to the country on that lovely sunny day.

But the driver's claim to knowledge of the way turned out to be a boast, and we soon got lost. There were a few discrete road signs but they failed to direct us to our destination, and so we began stopping to ask directions. Everyone was friendly and willing to help, but nobody seemed to know of Peredelkino, and we became more and more lost. We rode for a long time on an unpaved frozen road in the middle of endless white fields.

Finally we entered a village which was in complete contrast with the massive apartment projects growing on the outskirts of Moscow. There were low, ancient-looking log cottages bordering a straight snowy main street. A horse-drawn sled went by; women in kerchiefs were grouped near a small wooden church. It turned out this was a settlement very close to Peredelkino called Pavlenko. A five-minute drive on a small winding road through dense evergreen trees and I was in front of Pasternak's house. I suddenly recognized it on my right, a brown building, with bay windows overlooking the road. I had seen photographs of it in magazines.

Peredelkino is a loosely settled little town, hospitable-looking and cheerful in the sunny midday. I had been told that it was inhabited mostly by writers and artists, but most of Peredelkino looked like a settlement of small artisans and peasants—there is nothing "arty" about it although it is one of the most important writers' colonies near Moscow. The village has a large rest home for writers and journalists

which is run by the Soviet Writers' Union. Kornei Tchukovsky lives there in a cozy frame house where he enter-
tains his family and close friends on Sundays. Konstantin
Fedine, one of the best known of living Russian novelists,
has a house next door to Pasternak's. He is now the First
Secretary of the Writers' Union—a post long occupied by
Alexander Fadeyev, who also lived in Peredelkino until his
death in 1956. A long time ago, Isaac Babel was arrested
here. The house where he lived can be seen from Pasternak's house, lost in the snow beyond a deep ravine.

Pasternak's house is on a gently curving country road
which leads down the hill to a brook. On that sunny afternoon the hill was full of children on skis and sleds. Across
the road there is a large fenced field. It is a communal field
cultivated in the good season; now, in winter, it was a vast
white expanse dominated by a little cemetery—like a bit of
background out of a Chagall painting. The tombs are surrounded by wooden fences painted a bright blue, and the
crosses are planted at odd angles. There were brilliant pink
and red paper flowers on the tombs, half buried in snow. It
is a cheerful cemetery. Beyond it in the distance children
skated on a frozen pond, small, swift figures gliding in wide
circles.

The veranda on Pasternak's house gives it a superficial
resemblance to an American house of forty years ago, but
the firs against which it stands mark it as Russian. They grow
very close to each other and give the feeling of deep forest,
although there are only small groves of them around Peredelkino. Those trees behind low scalloped fences lend a
fairy-tale air to the lanes of the settlement. I was to find
out that while visiting in Peredelkino one is always taken for
walks on the snowy lanes. Walks are an established part of
life in Russia—like drinking tea.

I paid the driver and with great trepidation pushed open the gate at the fence separating the garden from the road. I walked up to the dark house. At the small veranda on the side of the house there was a door with a withered, half-torn note pinned on it saying, "I am working now. I cannot receive anybody. Please go away." After a moment's hesitation I chose to disregard it, mostly because it was so old-looking and also because of the little packages in my hands. I knocked, and almost immediately the door was opened—by Pasternak himself.

He was wearing an astrakhan hat. He was strikingly handsome. With his high cheekbones and dark eyes and fur hat he looked like someone out of a Russian folk tale. He was in perfect keeping with the tall fir trees and the wooden houses and the horse-drawn sleds. After the building anxiety of the trip I suddenly wondered why I had ever doubted that I would see Pasternak.

I introduced myself as Olga Vadimovna Andreyeva. Andreyev is a fairly common Russian name, however, and it took him a minute to realize that I was Vadim Leonidovich's daughter and that I had come from abroad to visit him. He greeted me with great warmth, taking my hand in both his hands, and asking about my mother's health and my father's writing, and when I was last in Paris. I felt he was looking closely into my face in search of family resemblances. He said he was just going out to pay some calls. Had I been a minute later I would have missed him. He asked me to walk part of the way with him—as far as his first stop, at the Writers' Club.

One walks into Pasternak's house through the kitchen, to be greeted by a tiny, smiling middle-aged cook, who helps to brush the snow off one's clothes with a little wicker broom. Here, one may take off one's overshoes and overcoat.

Then comes the dining room with a bay window where geraniums grow. On the walls hang charcoal and sanguine studies by Leonid Pasternak, the writer's father who was a well-known and talented academic Russian painter. There are life studies and portraits. One recognizes Tolstoi, Gorki, Scriabin, Rachmaninoff. There are sketches of Boris Pasternak and his brother and sisters as adolescents, of ladies in big hats with veils . . . it's very much the world of Pasternak's early reminiscences and of his poems about adolescent love. It echoes the world of *War and Peace*.

While Pasternak was getting ready to go, I had a chance to look around the room. From the moment I had stepped inside the house, I was struck by its resemblance to Leo Tolstoi's house in Moscow which I had visited a few days before. It had the same atmosphere of both austerity and hospitality. Pasternak's house retained what must have been characteristic of a Russian nineteenth-century intellectual's home. Both houses are furnished with comfortable but utterly unpretentious old furniture—both look like an ideal setting for a studious life or for informal entertaining. Needless to say, Tolstoi's house, although it was extremely simple for the times, is a great deal vaster and more elaborate than Pasternak's; but the lack of concern about elegance or display is the same. In Pasternak's own words, it was a house in which "simplicity argued with comfort."

Ten or fifteen minutes later Pasternak was ready to leave. We stepped out into the sunlight and walked through the evergreen grove behind the house in the rather deep snow which quickly managed to get into my citified Swiss-made boots. The sunlight had started to turn yellowish with the advancing afternoon, but it was still warm.

Soon we were on a country road where the snow was packed and much more comfortable to walk on, although it had treacherous, icy patches. Pasternak was quite tall and walked with long lanky steps. On particularly perilous spots —deep snow or snow slippery as ice—he would take my arm. Otherwise he gave all his attention to the conversation. He seemed to love walking. We took what was obviously a roundabout path to the Writers' Club. The stroll lasted for about forty minutes during which I felt an increasing friendliness on Pasternak's part. He plunged right away into an absorbing discussion of the art of translating, but he digressed from time to time to ask about the political and literary situations in France and America. He said that he rarely read papers "except when I sharpen my pencil and happen to glance over the sheet of newspaper into which I collect the shavings. This is how I learned last Fall that there was a near revolution against De Gaulle in Algeria, and that Soustelle was ousted. *Sous*telle was *oust*ed," he repeated with satisfaction, emphasizing both his approval of De Gaulle's decision and the similarity of the words in Russian. Actually he seemed well informed about literary life abroad and American literature interested him particularly.

From the first moment I was charmed and impressed by how much Pasternak's speech was like his poetry—full of alliterations and unusual images. He related words to each other musically, without, however, sounding affected or sacrificing the exact meaning. His word-sense was so inventive and acute that one felt his conversation was but the continuation of a poem—waves of words and images following each other in a crescendo.

Later in our acquaintance, I remarked to him on the musical quality of his speech. "In writing as in speaking," he said, "the music of the word is never just a matter of sound. It does not result from the harmony of vowels and consonants. It results from the relation between the speech and its meaning. And meaning—content—must always come first."

Pasternak appeared young and in good health. It was hard to believe that I was walking next to a man of seventy. There was something a little strange and forbidding in this youthfulness as if something—was it art?—had mixed itself with the very substance of the man to preserve it. Even his movements were completely youthful—the gestures of the hands, the manner in which he threw his head back. His friend the poetess Marina Tsvetayeva once wrote: "Pasternak looks at the same time like an Arab and like his horse." And indeed, with his dark complexion and archaic features Pasternak did have something of an Arabic face. At certain times he seemed suddenly to become aware of the impact of his own extraordinary looks, of his whole personality. Then he seemed to withdraw for an instant, half closing his slanted brown eyes, turning his head away, vaguely reminiscent of a horse balking.

In Moscow, I had been told that Pasternak was a man in love with his own image—but then I had been told so many different things about Pasternak in the past few weeks. Pasternak was a living legend—a hero to some; to others a man who had sold out to the enemies of Russia. It was his character Doctor Zhivago who seemed most controversial; many young people arbitrarily identified Pasternak the man with the fictional Yuri Zhivago.

In any event, I found that there was no truth to the charge that Pasternak was an egocentric. On the contrary, he seemed intensely aware of the world around him and reacted to every change of mood in people near him. It is hard to imagine a more perceptive conversationalist. He grasped the most elusive thought at once. The conversation lost all heaviness. Although he had seen my parents only a few times in his life, he remembered everything about them, their background, their tastes, their opinions. He recalled with surprising exactness some of my father's poems which he had liked. I soon discovered that it was difficult to get him to talk about himself, which I had hoped he would do.

As we walked in the winter sunshine, I told Pasternak what attention and admiration *Doctor Zhivago* had aroused in the West and particularly in the United States, despite the fact that the translation into English does not do justice to his book.

"Yes," he said, "I am aware of this interest and I am immensely happy and proud of it. I get an enormous amount of mail from abroad about my work. In fact, it is quite a burden at times, all those inquiries that I have to answer, but then it is indispensable to keep up relations across boundaries. As for the translators of *Doctor Zhivago*, do not blame them too much. It's not their fault. Like translators everywhere, they tend to reproduce the literal sense rather than the tone of what is said: in translating, it is the tone that is important. Actually, the only challenging translations are those of classics. It is rarely rewarding to translate modern works, although it might be easy. You said you were a painter. Well, translation is very much like copying paintings. Imagine yourself copying a Malevich. Wouldn't it be boring? And that is precisely what I have to do with the Czech surrealist poet Nezval. He is not really bad, but all this writing of the twenties has aged terribly. The translation which I have promised to finish and my own correspondence take much too much of my time.

"As you can imagine, some of the letters I get about *Doctor Zhivago* are quite absurd. Recently somebody writing about *Doctor Zhivago* in France was inquiring about the plan of the novel—I guess it baffles the French sense of order. But how silly, for the plan of the novel is outlined by the poems accompanying it. This is partly why I chose to publish them alongside the novel. They are there also to give the novel more body, more richness. For the same reason I used religious symbolism, to give warmth to the book. Now some critics have become so wrapped up in those symbols—which are put in the book the way stoves go into a house, to warm it up—that they would like me to commit myself and climb into the stove . . .

"Scholars interpret my novel in theological terms. Nothing is further removed from my understanding of the world. One must live and write restlessly, with the help of the new reserves that life offers. I am weary of this notion of faithfulness to a point of view at all cost. Life around us is ever changing and I believe that one should try to change one's slant accordingly—at least once every ten years," he added jokingly. "The great heroic devotion to one point of view is alien to me—it's a lack of humility. Mayakovsky killed himself because his pride would not be reconciled with something new happening within himself—or around him."

We had reached a long, low wooden fence, and Pasternak stopped at the gate. Our walk had already made him late. I said good-bye with regret. There were so many things that I still wanted to ask him. Pasternak showed me the way to the railroad station, very close by, downhill behind the little cemetery. A little electric train took me into Moscow in less than an hour. It is the one described so accurately by Pasternak in *Early Trains*:

> . . . And, as in church, I humbly watch
> Those I revere: old peasant women,
> Workers and simple artisans,
> Young students, men from the countryside.

I see no traces of the yoke
Born of unhappiness or want.
They bear their daily trials
Like the masters. They have come to stay.

Fixed in every sort of posture,
Sitting in groups, in quiet knots
The children and the young are still,
Reading, engrossed like wound-up toys.

Then Moscow hails us in a mist
Of silver-gray darkness . . .

17 / A Conversation

Werther has already been written,
But in our days the air itself smells of death,
To open a window is like opening one's veins.
—BORIS PASTERNAK, from "The Break,"
Themes and Variations, 1918

My subsequent visits with Pasternak merge in my memory into one long conversation. Although he declined to give me a formal interview—"For this, you must come back when I am less busy, next fall perhaps . . ."—he was interested in the questions which I outlined to him. Except for meals, we were alone, and there were no interruptions. Each time as I was about to leave, Pasternak kissed my hand in the old-fashioned Russian manner, and asked me to come back the following Sunday, so that for a brief period—three or four weeks—there was a pattern to my visits.

I remember coming to Pasternak's house from the railroad station at dusk by taking a short-cut near the cemetery. Suddenly the wind grew very strong—there was a beginning of a snowstorm. I could see snow flying in great round waves in the distant lights along the railroad station. It grew dark very quickly; the wind was so strong that I had difficulty walking. I knew this to be fairly customary Russian winter weather, but it was my first actual blizzard— *metel*. It evoked Pasternak's early poems, and the snowstorms of *Doctor Zhivago*. It was strange to step into Pasternak's house a few moments later and hear his elliptic sentences so much like his verse.

I had arrived too late to attend the mid-afternoon dinner. Pasternak's family had retired and the house seemed deserted. Pasternak insisted that I have something to eat and the cook brought some venison and vodka into the dining room. It was only about four o'clock, but the room was dark and warm, shut off from the world with only the sound of snow and wind outside. Pasternak sat across the table from me.

Although I was hungry and the food delicious, I found myself regretting the fact that I had to eat instead of giving my full attention to what Pasternak was saying about my grandfather. Pasternak had recently reread some of his stories and liked them a great deal. "They bear the stamp of those remarkable years in Russia, the nineteen-hundreds. Those years are now receding in our memory and yet they loom in the mind like great mountains seen in the distance, enormous. Andreyev was under a Nietzschean spell; he took from Nietzsche his taste for excesses. So did Scriabin. Nietzsche satisfied the Russians' longing for the extreme, the absolute, their taste for the grandiose. Music, writing— men had to have this enormous scope before they acquired specificity, became themselves."

Pasternak told me about a piece he had recently written for a German magazine on the theme of "What is man?" "How old-fashioned Nietzsche seems, he who was the most important thinker in the days of my youth! What enormous influence—on Wagner, on Gorki . . . Gorki was impregnated with his ideas. Actually, Nietzsche's principal function was to be the transmitter of the bad taste of his period. How quickly his aura faded! It is Kirkegaard, barely known in those years, who was destined to influence our own epoch. I would like to know the works of Berdyaev better; he is in the same line of thought, I believe—truly a writer of our time."

It grew quite dark in the dining room and we moved to a little sitting room on the same floor where a light was on. Pasternak brought me tangerines for dessert. I ate them with a strange feeling of something already experienced: tangerines often appear in Pasternak's work—in the beginning of *Doctor Zhivago*, in early poems. They seem to stand for a sort of ritual thirst-quenching. And then there was another vivid evocation of a Pasternak poem—like the snowstorm which blew outside—an open grand piano, black and enormous, filling up most of the room:

> . . . *could we be closer*
> *Than in twilight here, the music like a diary*
> *Tossed on the fire, page after page, year after year?* *

* From "The Break," *Themes and Variations*, 1918.

On the walls, as in the dining room, there were simply framed sketches by Leonid Pasternak. Half familiar faces of writers of the turn of the century looked upon us.

I had heard from people who had seen him while he was working on *Doctor Zhivago* that Pasternak rejected most of his early verse as too tentative and dated. I had difficulty believing it. There is a classical perfection to *Themes and Variations* and *My Sister Life,* as experimental as they were in the nineteen twenties. I found that writers and poets in Russia knew them by heart and would recite them with fervor. Often one could detect the influence of Pasternak in the verse of young poets. Mayakovsky and Pasternak, each in his own manner, are the very symbol of the years of the Revolution. Then art and the revolutionary ideas seemed inseparable. It was enough to let oneself be carried by the wave of overwhelming events and ideas. There were fewer heart-breaking choices to make and I sensed a longing for those years on the part of many young Russians. Was it true that Pasternak rejected those early works?

In Pasternak's reply there was a note of slight irritation. It might have been because he didn't like to be admired solely for those poems, or perhaps he unconsciously resented the thought that he could never write anything that could equal them. Or was it the more general weariness of the artist dissatisfied with past achievements, concerned only with immediate artistic tasks? Eventually, as I felt Pasternak's detachment from *Doctor Zhivago* at the expense of his new play, I tended to believe the latter.

"I have the feeling of an immense debt towards my contemporaries. I wrote *Doctor Zhivago* in an attempt to repay it. This feeling of debt was overpowering as I slowly progressed with the novel. After so many years of writing only lyric poetry or translating, it seemed to me that it was my duty to make a statement about our epoch—about those years, remote and yet looming so closely over us. Time was pressing. I wanted to record the past and to honor the beautiful and refined aspects of the Russia of those years. There will be no return of those days, or those of our fathers' and forefathers', but in the great blossoming of the future their values will revive, I know. In the meantime, I have tried to describe them. I don't know whether my novel is fully successful but then with all its faults, I feel that it has more value than those early poems. It is richer, more humane than the works of my youth. Those poems were like rapid sketches—just compare them with the works of our elders. Dostoevsky and Tolstoi were not just novelists, Block not just a poet. The voices of those writers sounded like thunder because they had something to say. As against the facile artists of the twenties, take my father for an example. How much effort went into one of his paintings! Our success in the twenties was partly due to chance. My generation found itself naturally in the focal point of history. Our works were dictated by the times. They lack universality now they have aged. Moreover, I believe that it is no longer possible for lyrical poetry to express the immensity of our experience. Life has grown too cumbersome, too complicated. We have acquired values which are best expressed in prose. I have tried to express them through my novel, I have them in mind as I write my play."

"Among your contemporaries' writings," I asked him, "whose do you think have best endured?"

"You know how I feel about Mayakovsky. I have told it at great length in my autobiography, Safe Conduct. I am indifferent to most of his later works, with the exception of his last unfinished poem 'At the Top of My Voice.' The falling apart of form, the poverty of thought, the unevenness which is characteristic of poetry in the late twenties are alien to me. But there are exceptions. I love all of Essenin, who captures so well the smell of Russian earth. I place Tsvetayeva highest; she was a formed poet from her very beginning. In an age of affectations she had her own voice —human, classical. She was a woman with a man's soul. Her struggle with everyday life was what gave her strength. She strived for and reached perfect clarity. She is a greater poet than Akhmatova, whose simplicity and lyricism I have always admired. Tsvetayeva's death was one of the great sadnesses of my life."

"What about Andrei Bely, who was so influential in those years?"

"Bely was too hermetic, too limited. His scope is comparable to that of chamber music—never greater. If he had really suffered, he might have written the major work of which he was capable. But he never came into contact with real life . . . Perhaps this fascination with new forms is the fate of writers like Bely who die young. I have never understood those dreams of a new language, of a completely original form of expression. Because of this dream, much of the work of the twenties was merely stylistic experimentation and has ceased to exist. The most extraordinary discoveries are made when the artist is overwhelmed by what he has to say. In his urgency he uses then the old language and the old language is transformed from within. Even in those years one felt a little sorry for Bely because he was so cut off from the immediate, which alone could have helped his genius to blossom."

"What about today's young poets," I asked. "I am impressed by the extent that poetry seems a part of everyday life for Russians. Large printings of works by young poets are amazing to a Westerner. Poetry in Russia seems very alive."

"Well, perhaps not as much as you think. It is fairly limited to a group of intellectuals. And today's poetry is often rather ordinary. It is like the pattern on a wallpaper, pleasant enough but without real raison d'être. Of course some young people show talent. Evtushenko, for example. However, as I was saying earlier, I believe that prose is today's medium, elaborate, rich prose like that of Faulkner. Today's work must re-create whole segments of life. This is what I am trying to do in my new play. But everyday life has grown very complicated for me. It must be so anywhere for a well-known writer, but I am unprepared for this role. I don't like a life deprived of secrecy and quiet. It seems to me that in my youth work was an integral part of life which illuminated everything else in it. Now it is something I have to fight for. All those demands by scholars, editors, readers cannot be ignored, but together with the translations they devour my time . . . You must tell people abroad who are interested in me that this is my only serious problem—this terrible lack of time."

My last visit with Pasternak was longer than the others. Pasternak had asked me to come early, in order to have a talk before a mid-afternoon dinner with the family. It was again sunny. I arrived at Pasternak's house shortly before he had returned from his morning stroll. As I was shown into his study, the house echoed with cheerful voices. Somewhere in the back of it, members of his family were assembled.

Pasternak's study was a large, rather bare room on the second floor. Like the rest of the house it had little furniture—a large desk near the bay window, a couple of chairs, a sofa. The light coming from the window looking over the large snowy field was brilliant. Pinned on the light gray wooden walls was a multitude of art postcards. When he came in, Pasternak explained to me that those were all sent to him by readers, mostly from abroad. Many were reproductions of religious scenes—medieval Nativities, St. George killing the dragon, St. Magdalene . . . They were related to *Doctor Zhivago*'s themes.

After his walk, Pasternak looked especially well. He was wearing a collegiate-looking navy blue blazer and was in a good mood. He sat at the desk by the window. I remember vividly feeling happy; Pasternak looked so gay and the sun through the window was almost springlike. As we sat there I wished our talk could be prolonged somehow: I was leaving Moscow the next morning. But the three or four hours I spent across the desk from Pasternak vanished like an instant.

On the spur of the moment Pasternak decided to tell me about the plays he was working on. Quite fascinated, I listened to him and only once or twice, unsure of some historical or literary point, did I interrupt to ask him for an explanation. The outline of the plays seemed bewildering at times because of the wealth of details which Pasternak provided to bring it to life. But I understood why when I remembered that Pasternak was Shakespeare's and Schiller's translator; clearly he wanted to write the plays with a German Romantic flavor and Shakespeare's uninhibited scope. He told me about it in concrete terms. He didn't emphasize the ideas in it but rather told it as a story, with an occasional gesture of hands emphasizing some vivid, slightly baroque detail. As he talked, I began to realize that parts of it were completed, others were still to be filled in. I was hearing about something which was not yet fully worked out in his mind. Like Tolstoi, he seemed inclined to give his characters a free hand in writing up their own destinies. Finally I began to see the underlying ideas. Although Pasternak didn't emphasize it, it appeared to me that he was absorbed in ideas about art—not in its historical context but as an element ever present in life.

"I think that because your background is so close to the events of the Russian nineteenth century you will understand the broad outlines of my new work. I am working on a trilogy.* I have about a third of it written.

"I want to re-create a whole historical era, the nineteenth century in Russia, and particularly the liberation of the serfs. We have, of course, many works about that time, but there is no modern treatment of it. I want to write something panoramic like *Dead Souls*. I hope that my plays will be as real, as involved with the everyday life, as *Dead Souls*. Although they will be long, I hope that they can be played in one evening.

"I admire the English for knowing how to cut Shakespeare. I think that most plays should be cut for staging. Not just to keep what is essential, but rather to stress what is significant. The Comédie-Française came to Moscow recently. They don't cut Racine and I feel it is a serious mistake. Only what is expressive today, what works dramatically should be staged."

"Did you have to do much historical research for these plays?"

"At first I consulted all sorts of documents on the nineteenth century. I am finished with research now. Anyhow, what is important is not the absolute historical accuracy of the work but the successful re-creation of an era. It is not

---

* It has been said that Pasternak was writing a play in three parts rather than a trilogy. To me, he distinctly spoke of a trilogy, but the concepts he outlined could easily apply to one play in three parts.

the object described that matters, but the light that falls on it, like that of a lamp in a distant room—or rather the inner light of objects.

"My trilogy deals with three meaningful moments in the long process of liberating the serfs. The first play takes place in 1840—that is when unrest caused by serfdom is first deeply felt throughout the country. The old feudal system is outdated but no tangible hope is yet to be seen for Russia. The second one deals with the 1860's. Liberal landowners have appeared and the best among Russian aristocrats begin to be stirred by Western ideas. Unlike the first two plays, which are set in a vast country estate, the third part will take place in St. Petersburg in the 1880's."

"Will this last play be about the revolutionary movement of that period?"

"Not primarily, although one of my heroes will be a terrorist. Essentially, what I want to show is the birth of an enlightened and affluent middle class, open to occidental influences, progressive, intelligent, artistic . . . But this part is but a project yet, while the first and second plays are partially written. I can tell you in more detail about those if you like.

"The first play describes life at its rawest, most trivial, in the manner of the first part of *Dead Souls*. It is existence before it has been touched by any form of spirituality.

"Imagine a large estate lost in the heart of rural Russia around 1840. It is in a state of great neglect, nearly bankrupt. The masters of the estate, the Count and his wife are away. They have gone on a trip to spare themselves the painful spectacle of the conscription, by means of a lottery, of those among their peasants who are to go into the Army. As you know, military service in those times lasted for twenty-five years. The masters are about to return and the household is getting ready to receive them. In the opening scene we see the servants cleaning house—sweeping, dusting, hanging fresh curtains. There is a lot of confusion, of running around—laughter and jokes among the young servant girls.

"Actually, those are troubled times in this part of the Russian countryside. Soon the mood among the servants becomes more somber. From their conversations we learn that there are bandits hiding in the neighboring woods— they are probably runaway soldiers. We also hear of legends surrounding the estate, similar to that of the 'house killer' from the times of Catherine the Great. This 'house killer' was a sadistic woman who took delight in terrifying and torturing her serfs. This incidentally is a true story. So extreme were her crimes that she was finally arrested—and this was at a time when almost anything was permitted to serf owners.

"The servants also talk about a plaster bust standing high on a cupboard. It is a beautiful young man's head with eighteenth-century hair dress. This bust is said to have a magical meaning. Its destinies are linked to those of the estate. It must therefore be dusted with extreme care, lest it be broken.

"Prokor, the keeper of the estate, is about to leave for town. He is going to sell wood and wheat there—the estate lives off such sales. But he joins in the general mood instead of going. He remembers some old masquerade costumes stored away in a closet and decides to play a trick on his superstitious fellow servants. He dresses himself as a devil with big bulging eyes like a fish—imagine something like a Chinese mask. Just as he emerges in his grotesque costume, the masters' arrival is announced. In haste the servants group themselves at the entrance to welcome the Count and his wife in the traditional manner, with marks of infinite respect, bows and compliments. Prokor has no other alternative but to hide himself in a closet.

"As the Count and the Countess step in, we begin at once to sense that there is a great deal of tension between them. We soon learn that during their trip home, an unprecedented incident has taken place. The Count was trying to get his reluctant wife to give him her jewels—all that is left in the family besides the mortgaged estate. As he was threatening her with violence, a young valet traveling with them took her defense. He has not been punished yet, but it is evident that after this action all is lost for him; it is only a question of time before the Count's wrath will be unleashed against him.

"The Count renews his threats against the Countess, and the young valet suddenly reaches for one of the Count's pistols which have just been brought in from the carriage. He shoots the Count. There is a great panic—servants rushing around and screaming—and the plaster statue tumbles down from the cupboard and breaks into a thousand pieces. It wounds one of the young servant girls and blinds her. She is 'the blind beauty' who will give her name to the trilogy. The trilogy will be called *The Blind Beauty*. It is of course symbolic of Russia, oblivious for so long of its own beauty, of its own destinies. Although she is a serf she is also an artist; she is a marvelous singer, an important member of the estate's chorus of serfs.

"As the wounded Count is carried out of the room amidst the confusion, the Countess hands part of her jewels to the young valet, who manages to make his escape. It is poor Prokor, still costumed as a devil and hidden in a closet, who is eventually accused of having stolen them. The Countess does not reveal the truth and he is convicted of the theft and sent away to Siberia.

"As you see," said Pasternak, "all this is very melodramatic, but I think that theater should try to be emotional, colorful . . . I think that everybody is tired of stages where nothing at all happens. The theater is the art of emotions; it is also that of the concrete. The trend should be towards appreciating melodrama again: Victor Hugo, Schiller . . .

"I am working now on the second play. At present it is broken into separate scenes. The setting is the same estate, but times have changed. We are in 1860, on the eve of the liberation of the serfs. The estate now belongs to a nephew of the Count. The new Count would have already freed his serfs but for his fears of acting too soon and hurting the common cause that has become Russia's foremost issue, her most urgent and complex problem. He is impregnated with liberal ideas and loves the arts. And his passion is theater. He has an outstanding theatrical company. Of course, the actors are serfs, but their reputation extends throughout all of Russia.

"The son of the young woman blinded in the first play is the principal actor of the group. He is also the hero of this part of the trilogy. His name is Agafon and he is marvelously talented. The Count has provided him with an outstanding education, completely exceptional for a serf.

"The play opens with a snow storm . . ." Pasternak described it with sweeping movements of his hands. "An illustrious guest is expected at the estate. He is no other than Alexandre Dumas, then traveling in Russia. He is invited to attend the premiere of a new play. The play is called *The Suicide*. I might write it," added Pasternak. "A play within a play, as in *Hamlet*. I would love to write a melodrama in the taste of the middle of the nineteenth century . . .

"Alexandre Dumas and his party are snowed in at a relay station not too far from the estate. A scene takes place there, and who should the relay master be but Prokor, the former estate keeper. He has been back from Siberia for some years. At her deathbed, the Countess disclosed his innocence and he was released. He is increasingly prosperous running the relay station. And yet despite the advent of new times, this scene at the inn echoes the almost medieval elements of the first play; we see the local executioner and his aides stop at the inn. They are traveling from the town to their house in the woods—by custom they are not allowed to live near other people.

"A very important scene takes place at the estate when the guests finally arrive there. It will include a long discussion about art between Alexandre Dumas and Agafon. This part will illustrate my own ideas about art—not those of the eighteen-sixties, needless to say. Agafon dreams of going abroad, of becoming a Shakespearean actor, to play Hamlet.

"This play has a denouement somehow similar to that of the first one. It is brought about by the local police chief, an obnoxious character whom we first met at the relay station while he organized the clearing of the snow by serfs drafted for this purpose. He is a sort of 'Sobakevich,' * and personifies humanity at its crudest. Backstage, after the show, he tries to rape one of the young actresses. Agafon hits the police chief with a champagne bottle, as he defends her. He has to fly for fear of persecution. The Count, however, helps him. Agafon goes to Paris to study. The melodrama of this part will be relieved by a domestic scene, gay

---

* Sobakevich is one of the characters in *Dead Souls*. This is how Gogol describes him: "No soul whatever seemed to be present in that body, or if he did have a soul it was not where it ought to be, but as in the case of Kashchey the Deathless (a ghoulish character in Russian folklore) it dwelled somewhere beyond the mountains and was hidden under such a thick crust, that anything that might have stirred in his depths could produce no tremor whatever on the surface." (Translated by Vladimir Nabokov.)

and tender. The adolescent children of the Count are assembled in their study hall in a state of high expectation, waiting for the blizzard to end. They are dying of curiosity at the thought of meeting the famous Frenchman, Alexandre Dumas. Their young instructor vainly tries to control their excitement.

"In the third play, Agafon will come back to Russia and live in St. Petersburg. He is, of course, no longer a serf (we are now in 1880) and has become an extremely successful actor. Eventually he has his mother cured of her blindness by a famous European doctor.

"In this part, Prokor is an affluent merchant. I want him to represent the middle class which did so much for Russia at the end of the nineteenth century. Imagine somebody like Schukin, who collected all those beautiful French paintings in Moscow at the turn of the century. In this play, the young teacher whom we saw during the scene in the classroom of the Count's children has become a terrorist.

"Since I think of these plays primarily in terms of theater, I am happy to say that I have begun receiving inquiries from theater producers. Right now, I just file them chronologically: the first one came from the Swedish Royal Theater. I am quite wrapped up in my plays—with only one thought, how to have time enough to complete them."

As we came down to the dining room, the family was already seated around the large table. "Don't they look like an impressionist painting," said Pasternak, "with the geraniums in the background and this late afternoon light? There is a painting by Guillaumin just like this . . ."

Everybody stood up as Pasternak came down. Besides Mme. Pasternak—Zinaïda Nicolaevna—Pasternak's brother Alexander was there with his wife, a gray-haired lady of great dignity. Pasternak presented his youngest son Lenya, a handsome boy, dark, eighteen or twenty years old, with quite a strong resemblance to Zinaïda Nicolaevna. He was a student in physics at Moscow University. Professor Enrich Nihaus was also a guest. He is a famous Chopin authority and teaches at the Moscow Conservatory; Mme. Pasternak had once been married to him. Svetoslav Richter is one of his most famous pupils. He was quite elderly and charming with an old-fashioned white mustache.

I was seated to the right of Pasternak. Mme. Pasternak was at his left. The table was covered with a white linen tablecloth embroidered with red cross-stitch. The silverware and china were simple. There was a vase with mimosa in the middle, and bowls of fruit—oranges and tangerines. The hors d'oeuvres—caviar, marinated herring, pickles, macedoine of vegetables—were already on the table. Guests passed them to each other as Pasternak poured out vodka. Then kvass was served, a home-made fermented drink usually drunk in the country. Because of fermentation the kvass corks would sometimes shoot into the night and wake everybody up—just like a pistol shot, said Mme. Pasternak. After the hors d'oeuvres the little cook served a succulent stew made of game.

At first the conversation centered around Hemingway. He was then one of the most widely read authors in Moscow and a new collection of his writings had just been published. Mme. Pasternak and the ladies at the table remarked that they found Hemingway monotonous—all those endless drinks with little else happening to the heroes! Pasternak, who had fallen silent during much of this discussion, took up Hemingway's defense:

"The greatness of a writer has nothing to do with subject matter itself, only with how much the subject matter touches the author. This results in a density of style, and it is this density which counts. Through Hemingway's style you feel matter, iron, wood . . ." He was punctuating his words with his hands, pressing them against the wood of the table. "I admire Hemingway but I prefer what I know of Faulkner. *Light in August* is a marvelous book. The character of the little pregnant woman is unforgettable. As she walks from Alabama to Tennessee something of the immensity of the South of the United States, of its essence is captured for us who have never been there."

Later the conversation turned to music and Professor Nihaus and Pasternak began talking about Chopin. Pasternak said how much he loved Chopin. "A good example of what I was saying—Chopin used the old Mozartian language to say something completely new—the form was reborn from within. Nonetheless I am afraid that Chopin is considered a little old-fashioned in the West. I gave a piece on Chopin to Stephen Spender which was not published." I told him how much André Gide loved to play Chopin. Pasternak didn't know this and was delighted to hear it. This somehow reminded him of Proust, whom he was reading for the first time.

"Now that I am coming to the end of *Remembrance of Things Past,* I am struck by how it echoes some of the ideas which absorbed us in 1910. I put them into a lecture about 'Symbolism and Immortality' which I gave on the day before Leo Tolstoi died. This must have been just about the time when Proust was first thinking of his book. The text of my lecture has long been lost, but among many other things it said that although the artist will die, the happiness of living which he has experienced is immortal. If it is captured in a personal and yet universal form it can actually be relived by others through his work.

"I have always liked French literature," he said. "Since

the war I feel that French writing has acquired a new accent, less rhetoric. Camus' death is a great loss for all of us. (Earlier, I had told Pasternak of Camus' tragic end, which took place just before I came to Moscow. It was not written up in the Russian press. Camus has not been published in Russia.*) In spite of differences of themes, French literature is now much closer to us. Only where French writers commit themselves to political causes are they particularly unattractive. Either they are cliquish and opportunistic or with their French sense of logic they feel they have to carry out their beliefs to their conclusion. They fancy they must be absolutists like Robespierre or Saint-Just. I mostly dislike those writers who make a career out of being Communists."

Tea and cognac were served at the end of the meal. Pasternak suddenly looked tired and became silent. As always during my visit in Russia I was asked innumerable questions about the West—about its cultural life, and our everyday existence. Lights were turned on as we drank our tea at leisure. I looked at my watch to discover that it was long past six o'clock. I had to go. I too suddenly felt tired and I had yet to pack my bags. I was leaving Moscow very early the next day.

Pasternak walked me to the door through the kitchen. We said good-bye outside on the little porch in the blue snowy evening. I was terribly sad at the thought of not returning to Peredelkino. Pasternak took my hand in his and held it for an instant, urging me to come back very soon. He asked me once again to tell his friends abroad that he was well, that he remembered them even though he

---

* But I met a Russian lady who was translating *The Plague* anyhow —"For the day when it can be published, and for friends to read in the meantime," she told me.

hadn't time to answer their letters. I had already walked down the porch and into the dark path when he called me back. I was happy to have an excuse to turn back, to have a last glimpse of Pasternak standing bareheaded in his blue blazer under the door light.

"Please," he called, "don't take personally what I have said about not answering letters. Do write to me, in any language you prefer. I will answer you."

18 / Pasternak Remembered

> *It has cleared its way*
> *And stares from the hill,*
> *Winter*
> *Upon my life through the frightened yellow leaves.*
> —BORIS PASTERNAK, from "False Alarm,"
> *Early Trains,* 1941

It is soft May weather in Connecticut now, but if I close my eyes I am back in Peredelkino; it's winter, I am sitting in the luminous upstairs study facing Pasternak. He is telling about his play, the passage of time suddenly seems arrested. I see once more his face across the wide desk, sharply outlined from the left by the light streaming from the window. Through the window fleetingly I glance at the hill with its toy-like cemetery. What queer premonition had led me there earlier that day—on my last day at Peredelkino? As I had arrived at the station too early to go to the Pasternaks' I went first for a knee-deep walk through this vision from Chagall, a hill planted with trees and crosses at random, the whiteness of the snow intense in the late morning sun.

I became reconciled with the thought of Pasternak's death for the first time when I received the following letter from a friend, a Moscow poet in his middle years. He knew Boris Leonidovich quite well. Last fall he went to Peredelkino on a pilgrimage and he wrote an account of it for me.

Moscow, November 1960

"A great deal has changed in Russia since 1917, but certain traits of the Russian people have remained. As contradictory as ever, they coexist in one person in unfathomable fashion: hospitality and rudeness, melancholy and gaiety, kindness and harshness . . . Certain habits too are unchanged, in particular a passion for travel. One need only walk into any railroad station to see a commotion familiar since my early childhood: sheepskins, coats, uniforms, suitcases bound with cord, food baskets, the air blue with smoke, and an endless, nameless crowd striving to get somewhere but in the meantime patiently awaiting their train. Through the drafty waiting room of the Kiev Terminal Pasternak passed nearly every day, rapidly dashing over the icy quay. In *Winter Expanse* Pasternak describes those war years when suburban trains ran right to the front which was closing in on Moscow, when it seemed that one additional effort by the German army was enough to lose the war. Pasternak remained among the diminishing number of those who believed in a Russian victory against all odds. It is in the course of those years that he truly discovered his country and he came to love Russia passionately.

"I buy a ticket for Peredelkino, the train is crowded. From the window the Moscow University building can be seen, and also the belt of newly erected apartment houses eight or ten stories high which have definitely altered the silhouette of Moscow as we knew it: 'Our cities find new faces sooner than the heart.'

"Little by little the landscape changes, wooded hills stand at the horizon. Beyond the window, a grove of small pine trees, sown some fifteen years ago right after the war. The trees, the height of a standing man, spread to the horizon in neat rank and file. A forest of tall evergreens is now coming up right to the railroad track, it covers a steep hill, wooden houses flicker between the reddish tree trunks, Peredelkino is near.

"Much of Peredelkino was once a large estate belonging to the Samarin family.

> *. . . cold and dark behind the fence*
> *A house whose beauty was marvel once*
> *Stands. The heritage of the park is old:*
> *Napoleon encamped here,*
> *Here Samarin the Slavophile served out his life*
> *and was buried . . .* *

"The 'house whose beauty was marvel'—the Church of the Transfiguration—is newly restored, its onion-shaped cupola now painted a vibrant blue.

"I reach the cemetery by walking along the railroad tracks, away from the rustic railroad station. Along the gleaming tracks up on the hill there is a switchman's shack

* From Boris Pasternak's "The Linden Alley."

guarded by a chained brown dog—underneath, the Pere-delkino cemetery.

"A protective wall always encircles the Western ceme-tery, but Russian graves are usually placed in complete disorder, while each individual tomb is enclosed by a small wooden fence as if to say: 'If there can be no solitude in life, let there be some at least in the hereafter.' Most graves are marked by crosses but sometimes one sees a red obelisk on the tomb of an unbeliever. On a little elevation facing south, beneath branches boldly spread out, a fence painted green encloses a large rectangle of earth—Pasternak's grave. It is covered with freshly cut autumn flowers, their slight smell acrid. Every day visitors bring them from Moscow.

"I must tell you about Boris Leonidovich's funeral: On a sunny spring day his open casket was brought here, car-ried on outstretched arms. On the eve of Pasternak's funeral, leaflets began appearing on Moscow walls, telling when the ceremony was to take place and how to get to Peredel-kino. They were torn off but more leaflets kept reappearing, particularly in the neighborhood of the Kiev Station.

"No Soviet writers of note were there, except for Konstantin Paustovsky. Mme. Ehrenburg attended in the absence of her husband who was then in Stockholm. The funeral service had sent a car to take the coffin to the ceme-tery, but Pasternak's family and friends disregarded it. The pianist Svetoslav Richter played a Beethoven funeral march on the poet's piano as the body was carried out of the house in a profusion of spring flowers, in a heavy smell of lilac, high above the heads of the crowd as was due to him. The great majority of the men of letters then residing in the rest home did not attend the funeral. During the procession I overheard a local Peredelkino *baba* grumbling: 'They (the writers from the Union) have not bothered to honor him . . . the cowards, we will not bother to go to "their" funeral when the time comes' . . . One unfortunate aspect of the ceremony was the indiscretion of foreign journalists who jumped up and down and swung around in trees in their desire to catch a more dramatic view of the funeral.

"After Pasternak's blossom-laden coffin was lowered into the grave, young men from the crowd started to read Pasternak's verse—they began with 'Hamlet' from *Doctor Zhivago* which was taken up in unison by the whole assembly. Young poets took turns reading Pasternak's poems and their own dedicated to him, others made short speeches.

"When a gaunt and poorly dressed man began a dull, religious-minded speech, the single official representative tried to stop him. A young man in workman's clothes pushed the representative aside, shouting: "Leave the speaker alone, this is not the Writers' Union here, you cannot stop us . . ." The poetry reading lasted for hours and hours, late into a warm May night.

"Down the hill, it is only a short distance to the poet's house. I walk along the fence of the Writers' Union Rest Home. Most of the wooden frame houses in Peredelkino belong to the Writers' Union and usually they are taken back from a writer's heirs two or three years after his death and given to another writer. Here is the gate which doesn't close tight, a graveled path leading to the house . . . In front of it, the earth of the vegetable and flower garden which Pasternak cultivated himself is now tilled.

"The house remains exactly as it always was. The guests are graciously met by Mme. Pasternak, and led into the dining room. Mme. Pasternak is restrained and dignified as ever; she has the calm and the matter-of-factness which helped her husband to survive a long era of turmoils. She goes out to attend to the tea preparations, I look over the familiar drawings by Leonid Pasternak which cover the walls.

"Later we proceed to the room where the grand piano stands. 'Boris Leonidovich was lying in this room during the last days of his sickness,' says Mme. Pasternak. 'The physician whom he especially trusted stayed in the house. Everything was done to lessen his suffering. Two nurses relieved each other constantly at his side. The piano was moved out while he lay in this room, but now we had it put back because it always stood there . . .'

"Through the window facing the couch I see a a maple losing its last leaves. When Pasternak last looked through this window it was May, the maple leaves had just begun to unfurl: spring comes late in Moscow. I go upstairs to his study following the narrow wooden staircase. Without him at the desk, the emptiness of the room is overpowering. On the desk lie some pencils, a fountain pen, a pocket watch, a small round hand mirror. Beside the window a bookshelf, Shakespeare in English, *Doctor Zhivago* in foreign editions, not many books in all. On a little table in a corner I see Pasternak's death mask under glass. A few black eyebrows are caught in the white plaster. The face is unchangingly masculine, magnificent . . ."

Only a year ago, the mention of Pasternak's name during a conversation with Soviet intellectuals would sometimes bring uneasiness, a slight embarrassment, especially on the part of younger people. Eugene Evtushenko, a great admirer of Pasternak as a lyric poet, told me: "*Doctor Zhivago* is not a good novel. It is dull . . . Zhivago is an uninspiring character, a selfish ineffectual man caught in events that he didn't comprehend. He does not do justice to the grandeur of the times that Pasternak undertook to describe. He is nothing but a worn-out bourgeois." This reflects the inability of certain Russians to appreciate a complicated, many-sided hero in a novel because their understanding of life on the whole tends to be heroic. This is not new, however. Dostoevsky's books were often judged very severely by his contemporaries for exactly the same reasons: lack of "goodness" in the characters, lack of dedication to a "higher revolutionary cause" on the part of their author. What indignation was aroused by *The Possessed* when it was first published! Many liberal intellectuals considered it wicked.

It is interesting to note, however, that Pasternak seems to have a growing popular following in the USSR. His funeral and the many pilgrims who visit his grave testify to it. Perhaps *Doctor Zhivago*, a banned book, has worked itself into the consciousness of the Russian people? There is a great power in a forbidden book. But there is a simpler reason for Pasternak's popularity in the USSR—the breadth of his personality, the ring of his verse. To his compatriots, especially to those unfamiliar with *Doctor Zhivago*, he conveys an image of transcendance rather than revolt.

Since Pasternak's death, there has been an effort to bring him within the realm of Soviet letters, as some of the declarations made by Soviet officials (notably Alexei Surkov) on the occasion of Mme. Ivinskaya's arrest indicate. For the authorities, it is far better to have Pasternak safely included in Soviet literature than to stress his nonconformist aspects by banning him. For his is a powerful voice.

One might think of Pasternak's funeral as a sequence, on a smaller scale, of Tolstoi's and Pushkin's funerals. Tolstoi's and Pushkin's deaths led to great manifestations of popular feeling—both their funerals were censored by the Czarist government. As many as 50,000 Russians payed homage to Alexander Pushkin after he died, killed in a duel on January 29, 1837. The vast majority of these mourners were illiterate; Pushkin's fame, his concern for the people had reached even the ignorant, poverty-stricken serfs. Push-kin had the reputation of being an atheist, yet many in the crowd were fanatically religious and there was a widely supported project to carry his coffin by hand to the remote village of Mikhailovskoye, where Pushkin's estate was lo-cated, and where he was to be buried. The government, however, feared an outbreak of popular unrest, and Push-kin's coffin was smuggled out of his St. Petersburg house and hidden in a church nearby. It was then taken at night to Mikhailovskoye in an unmarked carriage driven by police-men. Pushkin was buried there in haste—in the presence of a large police force and of soldiers.

When Tolstoi died in 1910, the Russian people as a whole went into mourning. Tolstoi had been excommu-nicated from the Orthodox Church for his heretic teachings and the government ignored his death, except for an effort at hushing the deeply felt popular grief. My mother, who was very young at the time, remembers the impact of the news of Tolstoi's death at Astapavo, a small railroad sta-tion where pneumonia struck Tolstoi as he was fleeing from his dissension-torn home. She remembers the news-paper headlines, people weeping in the streets, the con-sternation in her family: "An epoch is ended, the voice of our conscience is stilled . . ."

In his *Autobiography* Pasternak speaks of going to Astapavo on the day following Tolstoi's death. He went there with his father who was a close friend of Tolstoi and his follower, as well as an illustrator of his works. The small railroad station was mobbed with friends of Tolstoi, with students, with simple folk in tears. Pasternak describes how the coffin was taken into the railroad car as the people on the platform bared their heads . . . The train slowly started towards Tula, in the direction of Yasnaya Poliana, where Tolstoi was to be buried. (Tolstoi's home is literally named "luminous wood-clearing" in Russian). Pasternak's words echo what a half-century later his own death was to be for the Russian people as a great gap suddenly opened between our times and the fabulous Russian years:

> *The still ploughed earth, reflected in the glass of the railroad car windows, moving now, did not comprehend that somewhere right nearby her last hero had just died . . .*

Coming back from Pasternak's house on my last evening in the USSR I walked to the railroad station in the dark. It was a moonless night, and except for the main road to the station the lanes of Peredelkino were not lighted. The night was completely still, there were no snowflakes turning in the golden cones cast by the railroad lamps. The station's open shelter was empty. I waited for what seemed a long time on the snowy platform. Episodes out of Pasternak's plays filled my head, thrilling and confusing. At last I heard the train in the distance, its whistle echoing in the ravines as the huge red eye of the electric engine appeared behind a grove of pines. I hadn't even left Peredelkino yet, but already I felt a great gap opening between myself and what Pasternak represented for me:

> *The tales of our fathers, further away than Pushkin, the figures of dream . . .*

As I got on the half-empty train, I felt close to panic as if every turn of the wheels was taking me away from myself. I sat by a black window where I could see only the blurred reflection of my own face. I wanted to sit quietly, and I did not take advantage of the ride to write down Pasternak's last conversation. It was usually best to write down Pasternak's words at once, while my mind was still echoing with his broad and elaborate sentences, his clear voice, raised slightly at the end of each sentence. This time, the recording of our conversation would have to wait till tomorrow. On this last train ride from Peredelkino, looking around at my fellow passengers, I suddenly realized that I was no longer a stranger in Russia. My blue coat had grayed with wear, I had learned how to tie a scarf over my hat so as to be inconspicuous. No one looked at me.

As we neared Moscow the train slowly became crowded from making frequent stops at small suburban stations. Two women made their way toward my bench, laden with heavy sacks, each tugging a child along, a boy and a girl. I took the shy little girl on my knees. "What is your name?" "Aniuta," she said in a soft voice. She wouldn't say anything more. She had a fur hat which hid everything but her brown eyes.

A commotion started in the car. A drunk who had just finished a half-bottle of vodka right under our eyes couldn't find a spot for himself. A student holding a trigonometry book was particularly concerned: "Poor chap, watch out . . . don't drop your ticket!" The drunk stared with fixed eyes at the unstable world around him, his slippery glance couldn't focus on a single face. Somehow he got up from his seat, falling right back on his neighbor's lap, then he tried to get out of the railroad car on all fours. People held him back, no one was indignant:

"Poor man, he is completely gone, life can be so bitter . . ."

Filled with a feeling of unreality, I spent a sleepless night in my room at the Metropole packing and repacking my suitcases. How to fit all the notebooks, all the drawings I had collected? All the volumes of poetry? And the presents, lacquered boxes and small Ukrainian animals which had accumulated in my room? They had amused my young cousin: "How is it that your golden roosters multiply so quickly?" he had asked once. A golden cockerel, hero of a Pushkin tale, is a favorite Russian motif in decoration. I had several roosters and rams sitting on my dresser, not to mention the *babas* in bright skirts which had to be wrapped carefully; the unglazed ceramic from which they are made is very fragile.

Somehow everything was fitted in my bags as I left the Metropole in predawn darkness. Since Moscow University was on my way to the airport, I had arranged with my Intourist taxi driver to stop there on the way to pick up my cousin for a last good-bye. I spotted him in the dark, a tiny figure among the gigantic pillars of the university's front colonnade. Lost in early morning grayness the university was overwhelming in its symmetrical immensity: this was how Egyptian temples must have looked in their days of grandeur.

My cousin drove to Vnukovo with me. There we discovered that my baggage was frightfully overweight although I had given away most of my belongings—shoes, clothes, a few American books . . . Since I had already spent my last rubles on little jars of caviar and my cousin had no money with him, the situation was critical. I couldn't possibly leave behind anything that I had packed, except perhaps the roosters. Every object in both suitcases was essential, including a lot of materials on Soviet artists and writers. I was saved by the generosity of the airport employees, who after a short conference among themselves let me by despite my eighteen pounds of excess baggage. The customs people only glanced at my bags and I was free to go. A little DC-3 was taking three silent Danes and me to Copenhagen. The sun was rising; I felt terrible that morning. It is a burden to belong to two worlds at the same time, when those worlds which may be conciliated in spirit are politically at odds with each other.

I got out my notebook and began to record Pasternak's last words to me as we flew high over the Baltic Sea.

ABOUT THE AUTHOR

OLGA ANDREYEV CARLISLE was born and brought up in Paris. During World War II she lived with her family on a small island (Ile d'Oléron) on the Atlantic Coast of France. She came to the United States in 1949 as a recipient of a scholarship from Bard College, where she majored in American literature. Also at Bard she started to paint with an enthusiasm she still retains. Since 1953 she has lived in New York with her husband Henry Carlisle and their son Michael; before that, they spent some time in San Francisco. She comes from a family of Russian writers. Her grandfather was Leonid Andreyev, the playwright and short-story writer, while her father Vadim is a poet. Mrs. Carlisle and her husband are presently living in France.